PS RYDE

by Richard Halton

PS *Ryde* at Ryde Pier Head 29-5-67. Taken after electrification of the Isle of Wight railways. Note the ex-London Transport tube trains waiting in the pier head station.

John Goss LBIPP

PS *Ryde* leaving Portsmouth Harbour 16-6-68.

John Goss LBIPP

CONTENTS

Front Cover PS *Ryde* backing away from Portsmouth Harbour Station.

Mark Young Collection

Back Cover PS *Ryde* alongside Royal Pier, Southampton. .

John Goss LBIPP

Title Page *Ryde Queen* at Island Harbour 01-06-85.

Richard Halton

Above PS *Ryde* at speed.

Richard Halton Collection

Published by Mainline & Maritime Ltd
3 Broadleaze, Upper Seagry, near Chippenham, SN15 5EY
Tel: 07770 748615
www.mainlineandmaritime.co.uk   orders@mainlineandmaritime.co.uk
Printed in the UK
ISBN: 978-1-900340-94-6

PS *Ryde*'s passengers disembarking at Portsmouth Harbour.

John Goss LBIPP

PS *Ryde* moored off Portsmouth Harbour Station.

Nigel Lawrence Collection

INTRODUCTION

I blame my parents! An early trip by train as a baby and regular outings in the pram to watch steam trains at the local station (Wanborough) had a lasting effect. I was hooked! As steam dwindled on the railway my interest broadened in other applications of steam technology including paddle steamers and stationary pumping engines. I am not sure that I ever travelled on an Isle of Wight paddler. A family photo proves that I went on one of the Bournemouth steamers at a very young age (nobody could tell me which one though) and I remember a family holiday in Herne Bay, when I was about 15, which included a trip to Southend on PS *Medway Queen*. I do recall seeing the surviving Portsmouth paddlers moored in the harbour when I travelled to the Isle of Wight in the 1960s but my own journey was always on one of the motor vessels.

In the 1970s I was involved in preserving the Kent and East Sussex Railway and through that met Marshall Vine who later founded the *Medway Queen* Preservation Society. Of course my name ended up on a membership application form and here we are. A phased retirement (from 2011 to 2017) gave me more time to spend on PS *Medway Queen* matters and it was while researching that ship's story in detail for several publications that I began to accumulate some real data on PS *Ryde*. The two ships were moored next to one another at Island Harbour on the Isle of Wight in the early '70s but before that they had both been in the 10th Minesweeping Flotilla at Dover in 1940. Their paths must also have crossed briefly in 1953 when PS *Medway Queen* took part in the Coronation Naval Review at Spithead. Focussing on *"The Medway Queen Club"* for an anniversary book in 2015/16 uncovered more details of the *Ryde Queen*, as she became, and also introduced me to a number of contacts who have proved extremely helpful in researching PS *Ryde* and the *Ryde Queen Boatel*.

Researching a story is similar to investigating a family history. You start with a few general facts that "everyone" knows and an outline from previous publications. Then you start digging – metaphorically. Press archives are useful, the web is an amazing source of information on all topics although care is needed to avoid red herrings and inaccuracies. Web sites often copy one another and just because something is on more than one site doesn't mean it's the absolute truth. Local museums and archive collections have proved helpful and PS *Ryde* had the advantage here that her area of operation, except for wartime, was in a well-defined area. Even after withdrawal she was still in the Solent area although the formal archives carry less information about that part of her career.

This publishing project was sparked by a projected restoration scheme in late 2018. That, sadly, came to nothing and if the ship really is going to be lost then preserving the story is more important than ever. The encouragement of the Paddle Steamer Preservation Society, National Historic Ships UK and my colleagues in the *Medway Queen* Preservation Society has been very much appreciated. Hannah Cunliffe of National Historic Ships has kindly written the Foreword. I must thank the dozens of people who have helped me with information, anecdotes and images in the project. A book like this is never a one person exercise and without the help and interest of others the project would have got nowhere. Finally, of course, we have a debt of gratitude to the publisher who generously agreed to the request that PS *Medway Queen* should benefit from sales of the book.

Richard Halton

PS *Ryde* running empty.

Nigel Lawrence Collection

PS *Ryde* tying up at Ryde Pier.

Fred Caws

FOREWORD

The paddle steamer *Ryde* is symbolic of the British love of the seaside which stemmed from the Victorian and Edwardian era and the construction of the very first pleasure piers, including the pier at Ryde on the Isle of Wight whose foundation stone was laid in 1813. However, like many vessels of the Second World War period, PS *Ryde*'s career as a ferry and excursion vessel was initially curtailed. Only two years into her working life, she was requisitioned, painted battleship grey, renamed HMS *Ryde* and pressed into service as a minesweeper and anti-aircraft ship, going on to act as a guard for the Mulberry Harbours at Omaha Beach during the D-Day landings. In this publication, Richard Halton covers the varied aspects of her role excellently, telling her story from construction and launch, through to retirement and ultimate end use as a local night club.

Since their first invention, paddle steamers have proved popular and were built in large numbers of varying types which saw them used as ferries, liner tenders and tugs in addition to the more standard excursion work. Today, PS *Waverley* is the last sea-going paddle steamer in the world and PS *Ryde* is one of only ten paddle-driven craft listed on the National Historic Ships Registers in the UK. The technology which created these magnificent vessels has been supplanted and is no longer in common use, which makes the rare sight and sound of a working steam engine even more thrilling to those who have the opportunity to experience it and something that will stay with them for life,

even as it did for the young Richard following his childhood family outings.

Vessels that survive well beyond their expected lifespan are wonderful time capsules which remain in the memory of all who engaged with them in whatever capacity. In the case of PS *Ryde*, she will hold a special place in the hearts of many people, whether they built, travelled, served, worked or partied on her. The careful documentation and recording of these craft in volumes like this is vital to ensure that the stories and knowledge they represent are preserved, not only as treasured recollections, but so that future generations can understand and learn from them even if the heritage no longer exists in living form.

At National Historic Ships UK, an essential part of our role is in raising the profile of maritime heritage and ensuring that information about ships like PS *Ryde* is made available to specialists and the wider public alike. Through our three volume series *Understanding Historic Vessels*, we give guidance on how to best conserve these craft and, in the event that it is not possible to save the actual ship after all options have been thoroughly explored, to create a permanent record which reflects her significance. In producing this book, Richard Halton has done just that and has made a valuable contribution to the documentary evidence for PS *Ryde*, in a way which is not just informative but an enjoyable read.

Hannah Cunliffe
Director, National Historic Ships UK

PS *Ryde* leaving Ryde Pier.

Painting by Ivan Berryman

PS *Ryde* moored in Southampton after delivery to the Southern Railway company.

Science Museum Group

Refreshment Room entrance.

PSPS Collection

In 1936 the Southern Railway Company commissioned William Denny and Brothers of Dumbarton to build a sister ship to PS *Sandown*. PS *Sandown* had been built by Denny's in 1934 and launched on 1st May. She had been officially welcomed, as "the Southern Railway Co's luxurious new steamer", to her namesake pier on Monday 25th June by the Chairman of Sandown and Shanklin Urban District Council, Mr W J S Russell.

The new ship, to be named *Ryde*, would replace the oldest paddler in the fleet; the smaller PS *Duchess of Norfolk* of 1911 which was sold to Cosens & Co. of Weymouth and re-named *Embassy*. PS *Embassy* served throughout the Second World War as HMS *Ambassador* and returned to Cosens in 1945 where she took the name *Embassy* again and served until 1966. PS *Embassy* was scrapped in the following year.

PS *Ryde* was built to a very similar specification to *Sandown* and the two ships were visually alike. It was expected that PS *Ryde* could carry about 1050 passengers, a slightly higher capacity than PS *Sandown*. She was 223 ft long overall with a draught of 7ft 2ins. PS *Sandown* drew 7ft. They both weighed in at 700 tons displacement and both carried a crew of 30. PS *Ryde* was registered as 603grt which was less than PS *Sandown*'s 684grt. A memorandum issued within the shipyard by director Mr. E W Russell on the 16th October 1936 advised of the new order. It was to be a repeat of PS *Sandown* with Hull No 1306 and Engine No 1061. This was followed on the 19th October by a memo giving the location for her build as Berth No 6. The plan was to begin manufacture of the frames in December and begin erection on the building berth at the start of January 1937. Shell plating would commence at the beginning of February to be completed very early in March.

The order was placed in October 1936 and was for PS *Ryde* and another vessel (MV *Lymington*, delivered in 1938) intended for the Lymington–Yarmouth route. The framing was complete by 22nd January 1937 and the launching ceremony took place on 23rd April, St. George's Day. She was launched by Lady Walker, wife of SR General Manager Sir Herbert Walker KCB in the presence of her husband. Guests included Sir Francis Dent (a director of the Southern Railway Company), Mr R P Biddle (SR Docks and Marine Superintendent) and Sir Maurice Denny of the building company. The *Isle of Wight County Press* reported the event on 24th April with the prediction that holiday makers would welcome the new vessel with its full length promenade deck, increased seating accommodation and saloons. The provision of a "refrigerating cabinet" at each servery was greeted as "an extra refinement".

PS *Ryde*'s hull was constructed of Siemens-Martin mild steel with all materials meeting board of trade requirements. She had a double bulb angle keel, five inches deep, to reduce broadside drifting in a beam sea. The hull, machinery, boiler and equipment were guaranteed for 6 months after delivery to allow time for bedding in. The ship was supplied complete for her intended purpose except for drapery, bedding, glass-ware, plated-ware, earthen-ware, crockery, charts, chronometers and consumables. The decks were timber on the steel frames with bridge deck, promenade deck and main deck

constructed with four inch by two inch pitch pine secured by galvanized bolts. They were caulked with oakum and payed with marine glue. In addition the main deck was steel plated amidships at the sides of the engine and boiler openings. The deck over engine and boiler spaces and coal bunkers was to be laid with seasoned teak planks. The lower deck was of tongue and grooved white pine one and a quarter inches thick and three and a half inches wide. This was nailed to white pine grounds bolted to the vertical flanges of the beams. Access hatches were provided to the bilges for cleaning etc.

Bridge Deck

The bridge deck was not open to the public and was the nerve centre of the ship in operation. Storage for safety equipment was largely in this area. The navigating bridge had a wheelhouse and a magazine for flares and distress rockets, The wheelhouse was equipped with a Kent's Clear View screen with electric motor fitted and was supplied complete with signalling appliances, flags etc. Sufficient cork lifejackets for all on board were also supplied as was the necessary fire-fighting gear. There was a steam and hand capstan fitted aft and a windlass forward. *Ryde* was also fitted with an 11cwt bower anchor and davit and the necessary cables and heaving lines.

Cabin accommodation was provided for the Captain and Mate immediately aft of the bridge. The Captain's cabin was fitted with a sofa seat with sprung mattress and drawers under, cushions covered in approved carriage cloth. There was a wash basin with hot and cold fresh water supplied through nickel-plated taps. Numerous details were specified: chromium plated carafe holder and tumbler holder, brush and comb rack with glass shelf and metal rail, wardrobe with life jacket on top, bevel edged mirror, writing table with knee hole and drawers, bentwood chair with upholstered seat, stand-by bracket oil lamp plus hat coat and towel hooks. All-over carpet and a door mat were fitted. The sides were panelled in plywood and finished in ivory enamel. The window curtains hung on hardwood rods and metal rings. The door was secured with a Chubb lever lock and a slip bolt. It was also fitted with back and ajar hooks. Fittings were of Roanoid (an early form of plastic) and of polished white metal. The Mate's cabin was similar but with wooden racks instead of metal ones and a carpet runner instead of all-over carpet. Fittings were brown-bronzed brass.

Passenger accommodation is crucial to the commercial success of a vessel like PS *Ryde* and was provided over 3 decks; promenade, main and lower. The enclosed passenger areas were equipped with electric heating and the stairways built on a 40 degree slope and constructed of teak, with Ruboleum (rubberized linoleum) covered treads. She was finished internally to a high standard. The panelling over the steel work in public areas was designed to be removable and was fastened with brass screws. The first class accommodation was generally towards the stern and second/third class accommodation forward. Although a two class ship when built there seems to be some confusion over terminology and the lower rated accommodation is variously referred to as second or third class. The railways at that time ran first and third class carriages, second class having disappeared years before.

The First Class Saloon.

PSPS Collection

Promenade deck

The promenade deck had Haywards deck lights and there were two baggage hatchways on the forward part of the deck, each 10ft long x 7ft wide with pine covers. The deck seats were hinged to rails or were the buoyant type to meet Board of Trade life-saving requirements. Seats exposed to the weather were made of teak and well varnished. Forward was an open deck area with seating for second class ticket holders and behind that the second class shelter had garden type seats of pitch pine, stained and varnished with sparred bottoms and backs. There were spring blinds to screen the navigating bridge from the light emanating from this compartment and the sides were finished with a teak coloured dado with ivory enamel above.

The Purser's cabin was placed behind the deck shelter and fitted out to the same standard as the Mate's.

There were four lifeboats, two on each side mounted on the sponsons. These were constructed of larch planking with teak top strake; clinker built and copper fastened. Keel timbers, gunwales and rubbers of American rock elm were fitted, as well as copper buoyancy tanks and loose footboards. The boats were fully equipped and mounted on pine chocks on the deck. Davits were of rolled mild steel.

The first class smoke room and bar were situated aft of the funnel and at the stern was an open deck area with seating for first class ticket holders only.

Main deck

Forward was the bow steering gear and then the firemen's and seamen's facilities. There were messing facilities, without any sleeping arrangements, for six seamen and six firemen. There was no specific accommodation for stewards and waitresses. The crew's quarters were steam heated and equipped with their own separate galley with a three feet wide coal-fired range. They also had their own separate lavatory facilities.

The second class shelter on the main deck was situated between the forward stairs and the crew's quarters. It was divided in two by a screen bulkhead with 6ft openings on either side. The forward section was capable of being used by passengers or for baggage crates. The side seats would hinge up when used for this latter purpose.

The engine room gangways, on either side of the ship, gave access to compartments in the sponsons as well as providing an ideal vantage point for viewing the engine in motion – one of the attractive features of most paddle steamers. The Chief Engineer's cabin, similar to those of the Purser and Mate, was situated aft in the port sponson. The Second Engineer had a smaller cabin without a wardrobe and a desk without drawers forward in the same sponson. There were ladies and gentlemen's first and second class lavatories provided, mostly in the paddle sponsons, and all waste was discharged through storm valves in the ship's sides.

There was a galley and store in the port side sponson with a coal fired range, with one fire, 2 ovens and pan rack. There was a glazed sink with fresh and salt water supplies and the tiled floor made for a practical working space which was well-lit and ventilated. There was also a stand-by oil lamp and the compartment was finished with a teak-coloured dado and white enamel above. The 30inch wide steel door enabled movement of supplies.

There was a first class lounge aft on the main deck with mahogany ply panelling. The ceiling was not panelled but finished in white with exposed steel work cork-dusted. The seats were upholstered in moquette fabric. This compartment was equipped with cane chairs, hat-coat-umbrella stands and hooks. There was a small writing desk with chair and railway timetable racks.

Lower deck

Behind the chain locker and store was the seamen's cabin. Then the second class refreshment room with pantry and bar. There was seating here for 46 passengers, which does not seem high but the ship was intended for very short trip working. The tables were topped with linoleum and the chairs were bentwood type. Hat and coat hooks were fitted. Railway timetable racks were provided and there were stewards' store rooms and large wardrobes for the waitresses' clothing. Access was by stairs from the main deck.

In a space behind the refreshment room, with no public access, were the coal bunkers, boiler room and engine compartment. The boiler room was an enclosed space and the engine room astern of the boiler had public viewing access from the main deck gangways. Steam was generated in a cylindrical return tube marine boiler with a working pressure of 185psi. The boiler had 3 corrugated furnaces burning coal under a closed stokehold system of forced draught. A sea water cock was provided for cooling the ashes and a hoist so they could be removed and discharged over the side via a hopper. The self-trimming coal bunkers had a total of 50 tons capacity.

PS *Ryde* was fitted with a three crank, triple expansion, diagonal steam engine rated at 163NHP. Engine serial number 1061. The cylinders were 16in, 25½ and 41in in diameter with a stroke of 5ft 3ins. They operated at 280psi, 90psi, and 40psi respectively. The cylinders and liners were of cast iron and were securely bolted together. The liners were recessed at each end to avoid the possibility of ridges being formed by the action of the pistons. The pistons were of cast steel with piston rods, crossheads and connecting rods of forged mild steel. The engine drove the crankshaft, to which were fixed the paddle shafts each carrying a paddle wheel with 7 feathering floats measuring 14ft 3ins over floats when assembled. PS *Ryde*'s design speed was 14½kts which was achieved on trials.

Aft was the first class saloon, pantry and bar with a capacity for 54 passengers. Access was by stairs from the main deck. The saloon was panelled in plywood and finished with ivory enamel. The ceiling was the same as in the first class lounge. Hardwood tables had felt covers nailed to pine tops and the legs were attached to the deck with brass screw bolts and plates. Chairs were four-legged with upholstered seats. The shelf along each side of the ship was at the same height as the tables with linoleum and a fore edge on top. Bevel edge mirrors were installed and there was a secure cupboard under the stairway. All pantries and bars were fitted with counters and display racks, a cash drawer, bottle racks under the counter and a cash register. Roller shutters were also fitted in all cases.

Behind the saloon was a storage area and finally the main steering gear. The main rudder at the stern was steam powered and able to go between hard to port and hard to starboard in 13 seconds and was controlled from the navigating bridge. The bow rudder steering was hand operated through a screw gear linkage and controlled from the forward promenade deck.

The specification demanded that PS *Ryde* be finished with a black hull to main deck level, white above that. The funnel was buff and the ventilators white on the outside with red mouths. The bases of the ventilators were painted teak colour. There was a one and a half inch yellow band four inches below the bottom of the main deck moulding and a similar band against the top of the belting angle. Both bands finished in arrowheads at the stern. There was also a 3inch white band at the waterline.

She left the building yard on 29th May. Sea trials were conducted successfully and good results obtained with speeds up to 14.5 kts achieved on the Skelmorlie measured mile. The Skelmorlie measured mile (set up in 1866) is a nautical mile marked by two pairs of posts. The ship works up to top speed before reaching the first pair and, sailing on the specified bearing, proceeds from one pair of posts to the next. Timing starts when the first two posts are aligned and the watch is stopped when the second pair are aligned. The posts are mounted on the land, one behind the other, and observed from the ship. Each has a "V" or inverted "V" marker to show an "X" with its partner when they are exactly aligned. The ship makes several runs in each direction to obviate the effects of tide and wind. A nautical mile is about 1.151 Imperial miles, or 2025 yards, so 15.5 knots equates to about 16.7mph. The Skelmorlie mile markers still exist and are a Listed Structure in Category B. PS *Ryde* achieved 14.32kts at 53.1rpm and 14.768kts at 55.145rpm. The reported cost of the new ship was £46800.

After her trials PS *Ryde* was registered in Portsmouth on 1st June 1937 and sailed south that same day, passing through the Irish Sea down to the south coast and eastwards up the English Channel to the Solent. The ship was delivered to her new owners in Southampton on 4th June 1937, some weeks before the contract date of "end of July". Her arrival was reported by the *Isle of Wight County Press* on 12th June stating that she would enter service on 1st July and that she was the seventh vessel commissioned for the Portsmouth-Ryde ferry service in the past 13 years.

PS *Ryde*'s engine room. Although taken at a later date the engine room is one area that would have remained relatively unchanged after her wartime and post-war refits.

John Goss LBIPP

PS *Ryde* in pre-war service.

Science Museum Group

The driving force, PS *Ryde*'s paddle box.

PSPS Collection

STEPHEN CRIBB - SOUTHSEA.   SOUTHERN RAILWAY P.S. "DUCHESS OF NORFOLK."

INTERLUDE - FLEETMATES

The other paddle steamers in the Portsmouth fleet in pre-war days. Vintage postcards from the author's collection. Clockwise from top right opposite: PS *Southsea* (lost during the war), PS *Shanklin*, PS *Whippingham*, PS *Sandown*, PS *Portsdown* (lost during the war), PS *Merstone* and PS *Duchess of Norfolk*.

SOUTHERN RAILWAY P.S. "MERSTONE."   STEPHEN CRIBB, SOUTHSEA.

STEPHEN CRIBB - SOUTHSEA. SOUTHERN RAILWAY - P.S. "SOUTHSEA."

P.S. Shanklin 2411

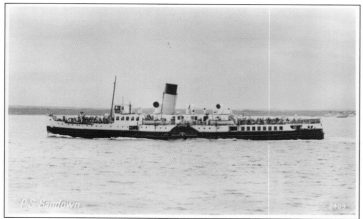

P.S. Sandown

Ryde Pier Head - 9

Ryde Pier from a postcard in the author's collection. Although described as "1930s" this view appears to be a 1940s image with PS *Sandown* moored alongside.

A pre-war view of PS *Ryde* heading away.

Science Museum Group

Approaching Ryde Pier, 1930s postcard.

Graham Shaw Collection

With the addition of PS *Ryde*, the Southern Railway's Portsmouth fleet consisted of seven coal fired paddle steamers of varying ages but mostly relatively modern. PS *Duchess of Norfolk* was withdrawn and replaced by PS *Ryde*. PS *Duchess of Norfolk* was sold to Cosens and Co. Ltd. of Weymouth who refitted the ship and renamed her *Embassy* as noted in the previous chapter.

PS *Shanklin*	(built 1924, 700 passengers)
PS *Merstone*	(built 1928, 723 passengers)
PS *Portsdown*	(built 1928, 723 passengers)
PS *Southsea*	(built 1930, 1183 passengers)
PS *Whippingham*	(built 1930, 1183 passengers)
PS *Sandown*	(built 1934, 974 passengers)
PS *Ryde*	(built 1937, 1050 passengers)

These ships remained coal fired until replaced by motor vessels. Although many other ship operators converted their ferries and excursion vessels to oil firing the Portsmouth paddle steamers continued to use coal. There was an Admiralty coal hulk (designated *C1*) permanently moored across the harbour near Hardway, Gosport. This was built in the early 1900s and was originally equipped with four cranes to handle the coal. As the use of coal for naval ships diminished the hulk was used less and in the 1950s two of the cranes were removed. It was eventually scrapped in 1964.

The railway owned steamers used another, smaller, coal hulk moored near the harbour Station. Designated *C11*, it had only two cranes from the outset, but was otherwise similar to the Admiralty installation. About once every two weeks it was towed to a railway connected jetty in the naval dockyard for replenishment. Coaling ship was a time consuming and messy business despite canvas screens installed to limit the spread of dust. Eric Walford who served on board HMS *Ryde* during the war commented that *"Being designed for the short voyage from Portsmouth to Ryde, her bunker space for coal was only about 50 tons and water not much better. Coaling on the Ryde was a nightmare. The coal had to be deposited on the bridge deck, then fed down a manhole to the deck below, and from there via a manhole each side, down to the bunkers. This gave the dust ample opportunity to get everywhere, but everywhere".* But despite widespread electrification of passenger services the Southern Railway was heavily dependent on coal for steam locomotives into the mid-1960s and conversion of the ships would have been uneconomic. Once the trains ceased to be coal-dependent the ships were too near the end of the careers to be worth changing.

PS *Ryde* entered service on her new route, Portsmouth Harbour Station to Ryde Pier, on Thursday 1st July 1937. The local press recorded the event with an extensive description of the on-board facilities that were described as *"substantial, tasteful and calculated to give the maximum of comfort to all sections of the travelling public".* This especially applied to the *"countless thousands who will obtain their first view of their holiday rendezvous from her spacious decks."* The paper also commented on the water colour prints of island beauty spots by Roland Maxwell that were displayed in the public spaces.

PROGRAMME

Thursday 1st July, 1937

Ryde Pier	dep. 11.30am
Portsmouth	arr. 12.0 noon

LUNCHEON ON P.S. "RYDE"

Portsmouth	arr. 4.20 pm
Ryde Pier	dep. 4.50 pm

The grand occasion was marked with luncheon on board for a contingent of invited dignitaries and other guests. Representing the Southern Railway were: Mr H A Short (Assistant Docks Marine Manager), Mr F V Milton (Superintendent of Advertising), Cmdr. Graham (Designer from the Mechanical Engineers Department, Southampton), Mr C T Pelly (Outdoor General Assistant, Southampton), Mr P J Harding (Advertising Department on the island), Mr C W England (Goods Agent, Portsmouth), Mr W H Pape (Advertising Department) and Mr H E Millichamp (Stationmaster at Ryde).

Other dignitaries included Mr H B Fowler (Vice President of Isle of Wight Chamber of Commerce), Mr A J Mew (Shanklin), Mr T J Fawdrey (Ryde Town Clerk), Mr R Lugg (Publicity Superintendent), Mr C A Ellery (Travel Association of Great Britain and Ireland), Mr F W Bradley (Collector of Customs, Portsmouth and Mr A Kinnear (Manager of South Parade Pier, Southsea).

After a toast to "The King" the guests were cordially welcomed by Mr Short on behalf of the Southern Railway Company. He told them that the modern passenger steamers of the Southern Railway Company had conveyed 2,326,259 passengers between the mainland and the Isle of Wight in the previous year. This being approximately nine times the population of Portsmouth at that time, and that the figure represented a 50% increase on the number of passengers in 1926.

He went on to say that the company was fortunate to have secured the name *Ryde* for their new vessel and that *"they were hoping it would be appreciated by their friends in that charming seaside resort and by the Garden Isle generally. Of the seven steamers in the fleet 6 had been built within the previous ten years".* According to a report in *The Evening News* there had been some difficulty due to the existence of another vessel bearing that name. This was thought to have been a collier working in the Newcastle area.

In Portsmouth the Harbour Station is a terminus built out into the sea on a wooden pier with the platforms end-on to the waterfront. Passengers can leave their train and walk down to the ships under cover without leaving railway premises. The Harbour Station was opened in 1876 as the terminus of the Portsmouth Direct railway line from Waterloo station in London. It was rebuilt in 1937 when the route was electrified.

At Ryde there is a traditional pier projecting out into the Solent but the train service (steam hauled in pre-war years and until 1966) ran from many parts of the Isle of Wight to Ryde where there were 3 stations very close together. Ryde St. John's Road served the edge of town and Ryde Esplanade was, as its name suggests, right on the sea front. From there the lines ran out on the pier itself to a Pier Head terminus. Alongside the railway were a tramway system for those not wishing to travel beyond Ryde, and a broad pedestrian foot way. The pedestrian pier came first, opened in 1814 and extended to its full length by 1833. In 1864 a second pier was built alongside to carry the tramway. Horse-drawn at first and electrified in 1886. From 1927 petrol driven trams were used until the tramway closed in 1969. The tramway originally ran through a tunnel to Ryde St. John's Road station, but when the railway pier was added in 1880 the tramway was truncated at Esplanade station and the steam train service made use of the tunnel. So, the Ryde Pier that knew PS *Ryde* was really a set of 3 independent structures.

The ferry service may have been primarily Portsmouth Harbour to and from Ryde Pier but some calls were made at one or both of the Southsea piers as well. There were also direct sailings between Southsea and Ryde. These piers were Clarence Pier by the fun fair and South Parade Pier which was a traditional pier projecting into the sea. Clarence Pier was more of a jetty or wharf with sufficiently deep water close inshore. There was no need for a traditional pier. It was originally constructed and opened in 1861. Although the pier is no longer in use by the ferries the fairground survives and until recently the "big wheel" ride was clearly visible across the Solent from the Isle of Wight on a clear day. Southsea's other pier, at South Parade, was a more conventional pier design and is only about 1.3 miles from Clarence Pier – a refreshing 25 minute walk along the seafront. Construction began in 1878 and the pier opened on 26th July 1879. After a fire in 1904 the pier was purchased by the Portsmouth Corporation and reopened on 12th August 1908. In 2019 the pier still operates as an entertainment destination although the landing stages are derelict.

The introduction of PS *Ryde* to the ferry service coincided with much publicised improvements to the railway timetable made possible by electrification of the Portsmouth-Waterloo route. The revised timetable improved the connection between the Isle of Wight and London and July also saw the introduction of the full summer ferry

The Southern Railway Coal Hulk at Portsmouth, possibly about to move for refilling.

Portsmouth History Centre

PS *Ryde* retained coal firing throughout her working life.

John Goss LBIPP

PS *Ryde*'s bridge bell.
Great Central Railwayana Ltd

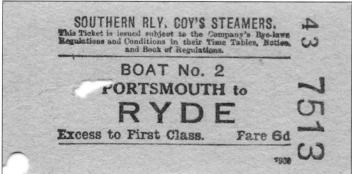

service. The ferries and trains together provided an important link to the capital and the new electric trains had been running alongside steam services, over part of the route to Guildford, since 3rd January. Some electric trains had run from London in May for the Coronation Review of the Fleet but the public electric service from Waterloo was inaugurated on 4th July when signaling improvements had been completed. The new express trains were made up of 4 car units with corridor connections (coded 4COR) and platforms at Haslemere, Havant, Portsmouth & Southsea and Portsmouth Harbour stations were all lengthened to accommodate the 12 coach trains in use when 3 units were coupled together. There were "4RES" and "4BUF" variants to provide catering facilities for the passengers. An interesting aside is that the configuration of the units' front ends with driver's window and route code board gave them a "one eyed" appearance. That and their destination of Portsmouth gave rise to the "Nelson" nickname. These same trains remained in service for many years, finally being replaced in the 1970s, a few years after the last paddlers were withdrawn. The 91 minute journey from London to Portsmouth and Southsea gave time for 2 meal sittings in the restaurant cars with diners changing over between Woking and Guildford.

Operating a ferry service is a matter of routine. A repetitive shuttle backwards and forwards across the same stretch of water day after day after day. The passengers regard it, perhaps, as part of the journey to and from their holiday as opposed to an excursion during the holiday which might be a well-remembered highlight. Even in the later years family groups photographed on deck are less common on the Solent ferries than on outwardly similar ships plying the excursion trade where a day out is the prime objective. This certainly appears to be so in the case of PS *Ryde* and her sisters. In order to get a report in the local paper a famous face had to be on board or something had to go wrong!

A famous face did appear when Haile Selassie, the exiled Emperor of Ethiopia, visited Osborne House on the Isle of Wight in 1937 while finding sanctuary in England when the Italians invaded Ethiopia. He and his family (wife, son and daughter) crossed the Solent on PS *Ryde* on 28th September and returned later in the day on PS *Sandown*. Whilst on the island the family took a motor tour to Osborne House and Whippingham Church before returning to Ryde, via Mersley and Ashey Downs, for the crossing back to Portsmouth. According to *The County Press* he found the Island *"very nice"*. He said it had been a *"very enjoyable trip and we have been most interested. It is delightful."* His daughter was at school in England and had stayed with friends on the island from time to time during school holidays.

In 1938 there was a definite preponderance of direct services between Portsmouth and Ryde, with few Portsmouth-Southsea-Ryde sailings. According to John Mackett's book, *The Portsmouth – Ryde Passage*, on a typical summer weekday there would be 14 ships from Portsmouth to Ryde, 10 from Southsea to Ryde and 5 from Portsmouth via Southsea. On summer Saturdays there were 28 ships from Portsmouth to Ryde, 12 from Southsea to Ryde and only 1 from Portsmouth via Southsea. Sundays saw 10 direct sailings from Portsmouth to Ryde, 10 more via Southsea and only one Southsea to Ryde direct. The frequency no doubt reflecting demand and the custom of taking holidays from Saturday to Saturday or taking Saturday day trips. As far as possible the ferry services were synchronised with the electric train service from Waterloo and the island steam-hauled services to Ventnor (via Sandown and Shanklin) and Cowes (via Newport). At that time there were many more railway routes on the island compared with today and services also ran to Bembridge and Ventnor West. From Newport trains also ran to Yarmouth and Freshwater. In the peak period there might be 12 trains per hour in and out of Ryde.

In August 1938 PS *Ryde* sustained damage above the waterline in collision with the naval drifter HMS *Sheen* at the entrance to Portsmouth Harbour. The paddle steamer was approaching Portsmouth at low tide and the drifter, outward bound, struck her on the port bow. Damage was minimal and a delay of only ten minutes ensued, none of the crew or the fifty or so passengers were injured. HMS *Sheen* was able to continue on her way and there were no injuries reported.

The ferry fleet operated a year-round service and spare capacity was used to offer the public a variety of cruises in and around the Solent. The trans-Atlantic liners operating out of Southampton were a favourite target. In 1938 the Southern Railway Company advertised a cruise on PS *Ryde* for Wednesday 17th August to witness the sailing of RMS *Queen Mary* for New York after her record breaking crossings. PS *Ryde* was scheduled to leave Portsmouth Harbour at 3.30pm, Clarence Pier at 3.45pm and South Parade Pier at 4pm. They would then proceed towards Southampton Water to meet the RMS *Queen Mary*. The fare was one shilling and sixpence. *"Teas on board the* PS *Ryde at moderate charges"* were also promoted. RMS *Queen Mary* had made her maiden voyage in May 1936 and had won the Blue Riband of the Atlantic in that year and again in 1938 and so she was still a very marketable attraction.

In December, a party of 35 disadvantaged children from Portsmouth, Chichester and Winchester crossed to the Isle of Wight on PS *Ryde*. They were heading for the Fairycourt hostel in Shanklin for a two week holiday. The costs were borne by the School Journey Association and the Portsmouth Joy Day Fund. A larger party was expected to follow them in the New Year.

As the 1939 season drew to a close the onset of World War II had an effect which boded ill for future seasons. The last sailings from Ryde Pier to Bournemouth before the war were on Thursday 31st August 1939, with the final steamer leaving Ryde Pier at 2pm. Thereafter trade from South Parade Pier, Southsea, virtually ceased and the ferries did not call again until after the war. The pier was partly dismantled as part of the anti-invasion precautions in 1940. A reduced service operated from Portsmouth to Ryde with fewer ships required and this was subject to gradually increasing restrictions according to the progress of the war effort.

The possible effects of air raids had been studied and it was not only from London that children and other vulnerable people were evacuated. After trial runs on 27th July the decision was taken to evacuate children and some parents from Portsmouth to places of relative safety; the naval base being an obvious target for the bombers. There was an arranged railway and shipping plan as about half of the evacuees were to go to the Isle of Wight, despite the presence of ship building and early warning RDF (Radio Direction Finding, later called radar) facilities there. Twelve sailings on each of 1st and 2nd September were scheduled but only eight took place on the 1st and five the following day. Some 5110 people were moved in this way. 76 patients including 40 stretcher cases were moved from Portsmouth hospital.

The wartime reduction in services to the Isle of Wight allowed ships to be requisitioned for other purposes. When they had gone the Southern Railway Company was left with the following ships to run the reduced wartime service: PS *Shanklin*, PS *Portsdown* and PS *Merstone* with PS *Whippingham* in reserve. Of these, PS *Whippingham* and PS *Portsdown* were requisitioned on 30th May and given naval crews for a short time for Operation Dynamo, the evacuation of the British Expeditionary Force from Dunkirk in May-June 1940. They were returned to civilian use after Dunkirk but PS *Whippingham* was requisitioned for the Royal Navy again later in the war.

HMS Ryde officer appointments

Taken from the Navy Lists 1940-45

The Royal Navy published a regular list of which officers were assigned to which ships in order of both the ships and the officers. No mean feat in the days before databases, computers and copy/paste. The National Library of Scotland has put the lists on-line as a series of searchable files. There are gaps in the sequence and the content has been auto-scanned; searching is by no means fool-proof. For each ship there is a list of officers with dates of appointment to that ship. As you might expect, the postings sometimes changed more quickly than the documents and there can be contradictions, but the appointment date removes most of the disadvantages this might have had. Unfortunately dates of leaving the ship are not provided.

www.digital.nls.uk/british-military-lists/archive/93506066

Appointment date	Name		Last record
28/03/40	Ty Lt.(E) J Boy RNR		02/41
30/03/40	Lt. J G Allen RNR	(Commanding Officer)	10/40
18/04/40	Ty Lt. A G S Curwen RNVR		06/41
08/05/40	Ty Lt.(E) A J Budden RNVR		12/42
01/07/40	Ty S/Lt H S Ward RNVR		10/40
10/07/40	Ty S/Lt. J J Roberts RNVR		10/40
23/10/40	Ty Lt. E T Symons RNVR	(Commanding Officer)	06/41
27/11/40	Ty Lt. A Jacobsen RNR		02/42
--/11/40	Ty Lt. A L Kirkus RNVR		06/41
23/12/40	Ty S/Lt. N A Jack RNVR		06/41
10/01/41	Ty S/Lt. D L Owen RNVR		06/41
10/01/41	Ty S/Lt. E H Jeffery RNVR		06/41
23/06/41	Ty Lt. J W Holgate RNVR	(Commanding Officer)	06/43
01/07/41	Ty S/Lt.(E) C B Dyson RNVR		10/43
30/07/41	Ty Lt. W N Bishop-Laggett RNR		02/42
12/12/41	Ty Lt. D Roe RANVR		08/42
22/03/42	Ty Lt. P V W Trist RANVR		06/42
22/06/42	Ty S/Lt. M J H King RNVR		02/43
22/06/42	Ty S/Lt. F R K Hare RNVR		08/42
28/06/42	Ty Lt. J Powell RNVR	(Commanding Officer)	12/42
07/08/42	Ty Lt. J R T Broom RNVR		12/42
02/12/42	Ty S/Lt. M S Joseph RNVR		02/43
--/06/43	Ty Lt. R W Furbank RNVR		12/43
--/06/43	Ty S/Lt. E G Walford RNVR		12/43
--/06/43	Ty S/Lt. C Rowley RNVR		12/43
--/06/43	Ty S/Lt. J M Price RNVR		10/43
19/07/43	Ty Lt. D J Beamer RNVR*	(Commanding Officer)	12/43
08/11/43	Ty Lt.(E) A J Panton RNVR		06/44
11/12/43	Ty S/Lt. R C Walker		06/44

*Eric Walford's account originally gave the name as Beamish, not Beamer, but these official documents and other sources say Beamer.

1940s minesweeping equipment as carried by HMS *Ryde*. This view of HMS *Medway Queen* clearly shows the Oropesa float, Kite and Otter Board used when clearing contact mines in World War II. This was standard equipment fitted to ships at that time. HMS *Medway Queen* differed in having a ship's derrick for launching the sweeping gear. This was a very unofficial modification acquired by the crew in Chatham Dockyard. Standard equipment was a boat davit or torpedo davit.

PSPS Collection

At the start of the Second World War the Royal Navy had a small number of purpose-built minesweepers and the knowledge from the First World War had been retained. In order to increase minesweeping capacity the Admiralty requisitioned many fishing boats and excursion paddle steamers to provide the numbers of craft needed. Training programmes were initiated and technical improvements made to equipment. The most common type of mine in 1939 was the contact mine with its heavy sinker resting on the sea bottom as an anchor. The mine floated at a pre-determined distance from the sea bed on a long cable and contained an explosive charge which would be fired electrically when a ship struck one of the detonator horns on the casing.

The antidote to the contact mine was "sweeping" to clear shipping lanes, using specialist equipment, towed behind the ship. There was a serrated sweep wire capable of severing the mine cables with an "Oropesa" float at the end. Below the float was an "otter board" to force the end of the sweep wire sideways away from the ship to span a swathe of sea. The otter also held the sweep wire down at the correct depth. At the inboard end of the sweep was a heavy "kite" to keep the sweep wire at depth throughout its length. Both otter and kite had inclined slats acting on the flow of water over their surfaces. Severed mines would float to the

surface and then be sunk or exploded by gun fire. When sweeping, ships displayed two black signal balls; one at the masthead and one on a yard arm showing on which side the sweep was deployed. The cleared area was carefully marked with "Dan" marker buoys by a ship assigned to that task.

PS *Sandown* was the first of the Portsmouth fleet to be requisitioned, on 24th September 1939. PS *Ryde* and PS *Southsea* were requisitioned on 12th February 1940. PS *Ryde* left Portsmouth on the 27th February for Camper and Nicholson's yard at Northam (Southampton) and PS *Southsea* followed on the 28th to the same yard. Both ships were modified in similar ways and this appears to be a fairly standard conversion for paddle steamers requisitioned as minesweepers. The aft First Class Ladies' saloon and lavatories on the main deck were cut back to increase the quarterdeck area as a working platform for the minesweeping gear. Boat or torpedo davits were added to handle the Oropesa floats and their associated equipment. PS *Ryde* had an enclosed bridge and wheelhouse so there was little need for modification there but an observation platform was added on the top of the wheelhouse, protected only by a canvas screen, and life-rafts replaced some of the lifeboats.

Her wartime complement would be far lower than her

peacetime passenger capacity so finding space for officers' quarters and mess decks for the various ranks of sailors would not have been a problem. Armament was added; usually for the paddle minesweepers a superannuated pedestal mounted gun on the foredeck and a couple of machine gun mounts for close in air defence. The large saloon windows were plated over and storage space was allocated for supplies and ammunition. Civilian colours gave way to an all over covering of battleship grey.

The final ship to be requisitioned was PS *Whippingham*. By the time this occurred PS *Whippingham* had already served at Dunkirk with a temporary naval crew. She was in dock in Southampton for repairs in 1941 when the requisition order was issued on 8th September. The work was further delayed by air-raid damage to the ship but in due course she joined her sisters as members of the "grey funnel line" and became part of the 7th Minesweeping Flotilla at Granton.

After conversion HMS *Ryde* (pennant number J132) under the command of Lt. (later Lt. Commander) J G Allen RNR, joined HMS *Sandown* (Cdr K M Greig DSO Rtd, Actg.) in the 10th Minesweeping Flotilla based in Dover. According to the naval movement log HMS *Ryde* left Southampton on 4th June 1940 and arrived in Dover on the 5th. In fact the rest of the flotilla's ships, including *Sandown*, were still at Portsmouth or Southampton at that time undergoing repair for damage sustained at Dunkirk.

In June 1940 the 10th minesweeping flotilla's composition was:

HMS DUCHESS OF ROTHESAY (Ty Lt J Dixon RNVR) at Southampton
HMS EMPEROR OF INDIA (Ty Lt Cdr B R Booth Pbty RNR) at Portsmouth
HMS MEDWAY QUEEN (Ty Lt A T Cook RNR) at Portsmouth
HMS PRINCESS ELIZABETH (Ty Lt W D King RNR) at Portsmouth
HMS RYDE (Lt J G Allen RNR) at Dover
HMS SANDOWN (SO, Cdr K M Greig DSO Rtd, Actg) at Portsmouth

Thus, in the early part of June, the flotilla's active strength was effectively HMS *Ryde*! HMS *Brighton Belle* and HMS *Gracie Fields*, from the 10th flotilla, had been lost during the Dunkirk operation. HMS *Medway Queen* and HMS *Princess Elizabeth*, arrived back at Dover to join *Ryde* in mid-June and by late June the 10th Minesweeping Flotilla was regaining its strength. Only HMS *Duchess of Rothesay* was still at Southampton in dockyard hands. An unsubstantiated report suggests that both HMS *Ryde* and HMS *Sandown* were involved in the highly secret "Solent Experiments". A whole raft of top secret weapons testing, many of which one could describe as Heath Robinson in nature. From dragged nets to capture torpedoes to some very optimistic anti-aircraft technology including the Holman Projector.

HMS *Ryde* and HMS *Sandown*, being well matched for speed (the *Ryde* being slightly faster), frequently swept together in an area of the English Channel which was a graveyard of ships which had been sunk by mines. They became well known as a pair and on occasion were allegedly claimed sunk by German propaganda broadcasts; but both survived despite several near misses. Diaries and accounts written by men on similar ships employed in this way suggest a lot of routine and frustration with more than their fair share of bad weather which must have been very uncomfortable in small ships designed for inshore work.

On Saturday 10th July, according to the wartime log, orders were received to the effect that the 10th flotilla was *"to be sailed as convenient for Yarmouth from which port they will be available for mine clearance operations as required by CinC Nore Command"*. In fact they did not all sail together as HMS *Medway Queen* was delayed in Dover by a defective dynamo. According to the movement log HMS *Ryde* was actually at Lowestoft on 22nd July and Harwich from 2nd until 10th August when she moved to Leith and then on to Rosyth.

In September 1940 the Ryde Townswomen's Guild wished to "adopt" HMS *Ryde* and a letter from Lieutenant Allen gladly accepted the suggestion. The ladies immediately started knitting so that the 45 members of HMS *Ryde*'s crew could be supplied with extra comforts for Christmas. This support continued through the war and was much appreciated by the crew; their letters of thanks were read out at Guild meetings from time to time. It is believed that there was just one fatality from HMS *Ryde* and that was Arthur John Carter, a naval auxiliary greaser aged 40, on the 22nd December 1940.

In January 1941 HMS *Ryde* was in the 7th Flotilla based in Granton, presumably still under Rosyth's command. By this time her CO was Ty Lt E T Symons RNVR:
The 7th Minesweeping Flotilla comprised

HMS PLINLIMMON (Actg Ty Lt Cdr G P Baker RNVR)
HMS QUEEN OF KENT (Lt N Psaroudis RNR)
HMS QUEEN OF THANET (SO, Actg Ty Cdr S P Herivael RNVR)
HMS RYDE (Ty Lt E T Symons RNVR)
HMS SANDOWN (Ty Lt H Runsam RNR)
HMS SKIDDAW (Ty Lt R C Jones RNVR, Ty Lt J A Harris RNR from 15 Jan)
HMS WESTWARD HO (Ty Lt G B Anderton RNVR)

On 15th February 1941 HMS *Strathugie* collided with HMS *Ryde* which was moored alongside the West Pier at Granton. HMS *Strathugie* was a minesweeping trawler, built in 1914 and taken over by the Admiralty in 1940. She survived the war and was returned to her owners in September 1945. HMS *Ryde* was docked on the following day with an estimated time for repairs of 14 days.

The ship was based at Rosyth until 11th March 1941 when she sailed for the Tyne, arriving on the 12th and remaining until 10th April when she moved to Leith. In July the same ships made up the 7th flotilla but several COs had changed, with Lt. J. W. Holgate RNVR in command of HMS *Ryde*:

HMS PLINLIMMON (Actg Ty Lt Cdr G P Baker RNVR) at Granton
HMS QUEEN OF KENT (Actg Ty Lt Cdr J Dixon RNR) at Granton
HMS QUEEN OF THANET (SO, Actg Ty Cdr S P Herivvel RNVR) at Leith, docked
HMS RYDE (Ty Lt J W Holgate RNVR) at Granton
HMS SANDOWN (Ty Lt D I Leake RNR) at Leith, docked
HMS SKIDDAW (Ty Lt R C Jones RNVR) at Granton
HMS WESTWARD HO (Ty Lt G G Anderton RNVR) at Rosyth

She then appears to have remained under the control of Leith for the rest of the year including a period in dockyard hands. HMS *Ryde* was taken in hand by Messrs Robbs of Leith on 22nd October 1941 with estimated completion by 10th December excluding trials. There is no indication of

The crew of HMS *Medway Queen* watch the sweeps to spot severed mines. This must have been a tedious task in cold wet weather.

PSPS Collection

Launching the Oropesa float and sweeping gear on a World War II minesweeper.

MQPS Collection

This diagram shows clearly how the various parts of the sweeping gear worked against contact mines.

*It previously appeared in "His Majesty's Minesweepers",
published in 1943 by HMSO and in
The Medway Queen published by the Medway Queen Preservation Society*

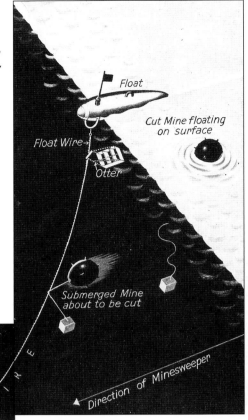

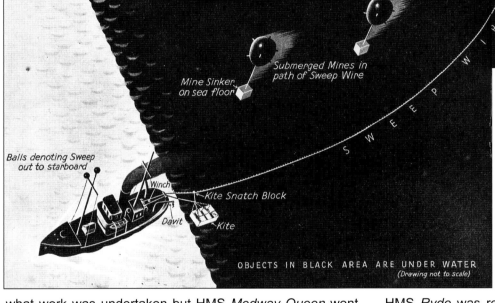

OBJECTS IN BLACK AREA ARE UNDER WATER
(Drawing not to scale)

what work was undertaken but HMS *Medway Queen* went into dock for a similar amount of time the following year for a major maintenance refit for which we have more detail and that included stripping and refurbishing the ship's main machinery. It is likely that similar work was undertaken on HMS *Ryde*.

In January 1942 the 7th Flotilla is reported as still having the same seven ships and all were based in Granton. HMS *Ryde* was taken in hand at Rosyth on 19th January for boiler furnace repairs which were expected to be completed by 7th February.

Although scheduled to move to Granton, HMS *Ryde* was taken in hand again by Russell's yard in Methil on 5th March apparently "due to weather conditions". She suffered another collision, with the drifter HMS *Lemnos*, on that same day in Methil Roads. HMS *Lemnos* had been built in 1910 and was requisitioned for harbour duties in 1940. She was returned to her owners in 1945. HMS *Ryde* suffered no damage but the drifter was declared seaworthy "only in calm weather" and Rosyth were requested to arrange repairs. The reason for HMS *Ryde*'s docking is not recorded but she left Methil on 8th March bound for Southend and thence to London where she seems to have stayed until 24th July 1942 when she moved to Sheerness.

HMS *Ryde* was re-fitted as an anti-aircraft ship bearing the pennant number 438. HMS *Sandown* and HMS *Whippingham* were similarly converted. These were coastal anti-aircraft vessels which operated independently with a view to shooting down Luftwaffe aircraft. The minesweeping gear was removed and her anti-aircraft armament considerably increased. She would now carry three Pompom weapons, four Oerlikon cannon and 2 Boulton Paul power operated turrets, she also had searchlights, Lewis guns and a twin rocket launcher. The Boulton Paul turrets were the type fitted to the Defiant aircraft in the early part of the war and each mounted four .303 machine guns. The turrets were power operated to track the target aircraft. The Navy Lists suggest that there were a number of new officer appointments in June 1942, including S/Lt M King (see below) and Lt. J Powell RNVR (Commanding Officer), consistent with taking up her new role.

We are fortunate to have two first-hand accounts of life on board HMS *Ryde* during her time as an anti-aircraft vessel. The first by Michael King, who served on board for a fairly short time when the ship was an AA vessel and included the following account of some of the lighter moments in her routine. The timescales suggest that he came on board very soon after her conversion. On the 24th

July 1942 she was at Sheerness when Sub Lt. Michael King joined her. Life on board was certainly varied as can be seen in his account:

"I was drafted to a ship called HMS Ryde, a paddle ship. This was also in Sheerness. This ship in civil life had plied between Portsmouth and the Isle of Wight as a pleasure craft but now her decks were stuffed with antiaircraft armament which consisted of a 12 pounder fore and aft, Oerlikons, pompoms and two Boulton Paul turrets. These turrets each contained four very rapid fire machine guns and had been taken from Royal Air Force planes which were no longer in service. She was manned by five officers, the commanding officer who was a Lt Commander, the 1st Lt who was a Lt, all RNVR, the engineer who was also a Lt RNR, having come straight from the merchant services, and two sub lieutenants, one of whom was of the same rank as me but junior to me.

I was gunnery officer. Our duties consisted of putting up a barrage of fire when enemy aircraft flew low over the coast and for this purpose we patrolled up and down the coast outside Sheerness. Our duties were not very onerous except the junior sub-Lt and I were required to keep alternative watches, the other officers remaining peacefully asleep in their bunks. If anything untoward happened they would appear. This was the captain's idea and, quite frankly, my opposite number and I became very tired after a month of this due to lack of sleep. I developed sinus trouble and had to go ashore to the doctor to have my sinuses cauterised which consisted in those days of metal rods which were heated being put up one's nostrils, the clouds of burning flesh were a bit alarming but it didn't last long and I didn't get any leave. However, I had to go and see the Senior Naval Officer in command of Sheerness, a very nice chap called Capt. Cordaux and whilst having a chat with him I mentioned that the other sub-Lt and I were keeping watch and watch. He was most surprised at this and reprimanded my commanding officer. He asked me if I would like a draft elsewhere to which I replied in the affirmative. However the CO and I parted on very amicable terms and in fact years later I met him out in the Far East and we had a drinking session together.

Before leaving HMS Ryde I ought to mention some happenings which have stuck in my mind. Occasionally my parents came to Sheerness and stayed in the Fountain Hotel so that I could see them when the ship came in, which was fairly frequent. That was nice. I met a very pretty girl with whom I became friendly. She was on the quayside when I first saw her and so I addressed her as Nellie and she wanted to know how I knew her name. That was easy – she had a name tab on her gloves, one of which was showing. We were great friends from then on and I used to take her out when I had shore leave. The other sub-Lt aboard was an Australian, a pimply youth who thought he was God's gift to all women and he used to compare English girls unfavourably with Australians. I hit on the idea of letting him meet a really pretty English girl and so I started a course of correspondence with him in disguised handwriting and I dabbed the notepaper

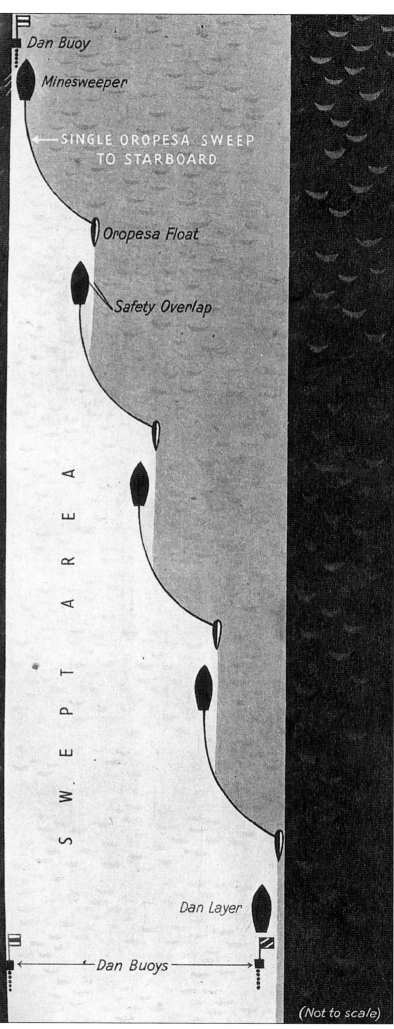

Sub Lt. Michael King.

Courtesy of his son, Chris.

and envelopes with rather loud smelling hair oil to give the impression of perfume, handed the missive to the steward who gave it to him saying a very pretty young girl in Wren uniform had left it.

In the first such letter I wrote "I have seen you about the place and I think you look marvellous. Possibly we could meet somewhere? I don't want to be too forward but do please reply" and I signed it with best wishes from Biddy Smeller. I put the address of the local Wren hostelry on the 21 notepaper. I had already arranged with Nellie who was a WRN and who lived at the address to get his replies, if any, and to let me have them. He reacted beautifully and I kept up the correspondence in this way and whenever he got a letter he would smell the envelope and with a gasp say "Ah Biddy" and would tell the rest of us what he would do when he met her.

After a week or so of this I decided the time had come when he should in fact meet "Biddy". I borrowed a Wren uniform from one of Nellie's friends and she and I and her friend waited in her room for the sub-lieutenant to appear, which he did on the dot. It was in the evening and there was a subdued light in the room so that I shouldn't be recognised too easily and Nellie and her friend went behind the scenes when the doorbell rang. I called out in a treble voice "do come in" and he did so making a beeline for me. I got up from the sofa where I had been lying languidly, threw my arms round his neck and plastered his face with cupid bow kisses. He looked rather surprised momentarily and then he started to come for me so I gave him a little push on his chest saying "Oh this is so sudden" and being a small chap he reeled backwards and sat on the floor, at which point the girls came in and we had a jolly good party. He took it very well but after that he never did swank about his prowess with English girls again.

Another officer aboard the Ryde had a bit of a drink problem. So much so that on one occasion when I knew he

had had too much at lunchtime and we were in port, I put a plate lifter under the tablecloth and under his plate of soup. When he sat down I squeezed the bulb and his plate started going up and down. He never said a word. He looked at it in horror and got up and went out of the wardroom and signed the pledge.

Now and again when we were in port and off duty we had a party in the wardroom. These parties were fairly hilarious. One game we played was called 'The Bounding boys of the Bosphorus'. This consisted of piling up all the chairs and tables upside down with their legs sticking up at the far end of the wardroom. We would then take turns in running towards these chairs and tables and diving over the top of them, yelling out as we did so "I am a bounding boy of the Bosphorous". The object of the game was to see who could clear the chairs and tables without touching them, turn a somersault the far end and regain one's feet. This was quite difficult but we never seemed to hurt ourselves."

After HMS *Ryde*, Michael King went to admiralty trawler HMS *Great Admiral* which was in use as an Auxiliary Patrol Vessel in the Iceland command. By September 1943 he was in command of another trawler, HMS *Fiaray*.

HMS *Ryde* was alongside in Chatham from 31st October until 20th November 1942 and appears to have spent the first half of 1943 having her boiler problems corrected. Repairs were tried at Sheerness/Queenborough in January but in April she was taken into Chatham Dockyard again for fitting of a new boiler. This was supposed to be completed in July and the ship became part of the Thames Local Defence Flotilla as Eric Walford notes below. This perhaps explains another flurry of new officer appointments in June 1943.

Our second account of life on board is from Eric Walford, who was also gunnery officer (appointed in June 1943) and who remained on board for the rest of HMS *Ryde*'s commission. He joined while the ship was in Chatham having a replacement boiler fitted. Lt. J Powell RNVR was superseded as CO by Lt. D J Beamer RNVR in July 1943.

Eric Walford recorded: "I was serving in a paddle steamer called HMS *Jeanie Deans*, as a Sub-Lieutenant RNVR. Wishing for a more warlike vessel, I went up to the Admiralty to request I be appointed to destroyers. We were at the time lying in Chatham Dockyard for a boiler clean, which is why I was able to get the time to go to London. The very next day, some of the crew asked me if the rumour they had heard was true. Was I going to join HMS *Ryde* as Gunnery officer? The Ryde at the time was lying across the basin, having a new boiler installed. I explained that I had just been to the Admiralty requesting destroyers and no way would I be joining the Ryde.

My next appointment came through a few days later – and I was appointed to HMS *Ryde*! Now in those days, only three officers were nominated for specific jobs: The Commanding Officer, the First Lieutenant, and the Chief Engineer. Three more officers were appointed for watch-keeping duties, their other specific duties being rather a case of 'eenie meenie minee mo'. And guess who got the job of Gunnery Officer? Since that time, I have never totally discounted a rumour! The CO was Lieutenant Beamer, the First Lieutenant, R Furbank and the Chief Engineer Lieutenant Dyson RNR. Other officers were Sub Lieutenant Charley Rowley and another Sub Lieutenant whose name escapes me.

At first, we became part of the Thames Local Defence Flotilla (TLDF), which were Anti-Aircraft vessels, armed with two 2-pounder pom-poms, three 20mm Oerlikons, and two ex-aircraft four barrelled Browning machine gun hydraulic turrets. Our duties were to anchor out in the estuary, as anti-aircraft guard ships. . Accommodation was relatively spacious, and even I had two cabins, one of which was on the after-end of the bridge, which I later turned into an aircraft recognition room."

On 29th October HMS *Ryde* arrived for duty at Harwich and for the next few months she was based there with a couple of weeks in Lowestoft in January/February 1944.

Eric Walford again: *"Not long after joining the Ryde, she was moved to Harwich to operate from there. Many times we would be anchored off the Cork Light vessel for a night or two. Our berth in Harwich was inside the arms of the train-loading piers. One memorable night in Harwich, we opened fire on a German aircraft, which resulted in one crew member being injured by a piece of shrapnel – from one of our own guns, as it turned out. The safety rails to prevent firing into any of the superstructure had, it appeared, been fitted before the halliards were rigged, and a shell from one of the Oerlikons had struck a halliard and exploded. Quite how I escaped, I have no idea, as I was standing on the wing of the bridge at the time."*

On 29th February HMS *Ryde* left Harwich and moved to Southend, presumably guarding the Thames again, and was then moved to Portsmouth on or about the 27th May. There she prepared for her role as an anti-aircraft defence ship for "Mulberry A", one of the temporary harbours constructed off the invasion beaches for the landing of supplies.

The first contingent of Mulberry Harbour forces were ordered to sail in the afternoon of 6th June. They were headed for Arromanches, designated site for "Mulberry B" under British control. The headquarters personnel were first across in HMS *Aristocrat* a Clyde paddler converted as an AA vessel. HMS *Aristocrat* was unusual in that her propulsion system was diesel-electric. HMS *Sandown* was a control vessel at Mulberry B from 11th to 20th June and HMS *Whippingham* was also involved in the air defence force.

According to the movement log HMS *Ryde* left Portsmouth on 12th June 1944. She was part of a convoy heading for Omaha beach and "Mulberry A" which was under construction and which would be under American control. The harbour would be sited below the villages of Colleville, St. Laurent and Vierville. There were a succession of convoys to each of the Mulberry harbours; delivering components and other material as required. The first components of Mulberry A arrived on 9th June while the area was still in range of German snipers. The start of construction was delayed until 12th June. HMS *Ryde* was one of a number of AA ships intended for harbour defence while the Mulberry was being assembled and when in use. As such she was not counted as part of the convoy defence screen which was provided by a flotilla of destroyers and corvettes. The first Sherman tank trundled carefully ashore on 16th June. Some components had been lost during the tows and a number of the pontoons supporting the floating piers had a lower design load capability than the weight of a tank!

Eric Walford: *"In May 1944, we were sailing to Portsmouth to join the invasion fleet, designated as an anti-aircraft guard ship for Mulberry A, at the Omaha Beachhead. For some odd reason, we were not sailed with the main force, but just a few days later. On arrival, we were instructed to anchor off the Western side of the Mulberry. The Ryde had only been fitted with one anchor, as anchoring often was not envisaged when she was first built. When we anchored off the Mulberry, the Ryde dragged her anchor towards the shore until quite close to the shore, and then it held. No matter how often we re-anchored, the result was the same, and we ended up quite close inshore, with the stern towards the shore.*

One night, shortly after taking up position, the first doodlebug we ever saw passed over the beachhead, to be met by an absolute hail of fire from the trigger-happy Americans, but it sailed on untouched. Strange to say, it was heading inland to France. We were sent some American SeaBees to accommodate, and I well remember being called to the main deck, where one of these was lying on his camp bed, rolling a 20mm Oerlikon shell with his finger. The shell had come through the wooden deck and, fortunately, had failed to explode. I picked it up and floated it over the side."

The Germans had realised what was going on by this time and air attacks, mostly by mine-laying aircraft began. The AA barrage was intense and, in the tradition of such measures, inclined to open up on any aircraft without checking identification. Construction continued but on 19th June the weather deteriorated and the wind strength increased. The storm lasted for several days and at Mulberry A the harbour including the breakwater of immense concrete "Phoenix" Caissons and block ships was badly damaged. Mulberry B was in a more sheltered position and fared better so the decision was taken to use parts of Mulberry A to repair B. The American harbour was abandoned but the breakwaters were strengthened to shelter the beaches where stores were still being landed.

In a post-war press report Lt. Beamer recalled *"We were on guard ship duty during the building of the Mulberry Harbour. By that time German air power had been snuffed out so we were a flak ship that didn't have to let off any flak. We did have a bad moment though when the northerly gale smashed up the Mulberry Harbour. To avoid grounding we had to steam clear of the coast and my big worry was saving the paddles from being damaged by floating wreckage. It took the ship four hours to get clear. When the gale abated she headed back – and was blown to her original location in 20 minutes. I was amazed at the way she rode that gale, even if she did behave like an old duck. She was an ideal flak ship too because of her broad beam."*

Eric Walford: *"We remained at Omaha until after the storm which did so much damage, and then we were told, "If you have enough coal, return to Portsmouth, if you do not have enough coal, run the ship onto the beach!" We arrived back in Portsmouth sweeping out the bunkers! After bunkering and filling up with water, we became part of the anti-doodlebug guard for Portsmouth, anchoring off Bembridge – for eight weeks with no mail - AND we never saw another doodlebug, so we must have scared them away. In August we were told that the ship was to be returned to her civilian owners - the Southern Railway - and we took the ship to somewhere near Warsash and paid her off."*

HMS *Ryde*'s naval movement log ends with the undated statement "As "R" will no longer be required by C in C Portsmouth for anti-flying bomb duties she can be released from Overlord". By deduction from reports of her re-entry into service it would seem that she was handed back to her civilian owners in February or March of 1945.

Rod Williams' painting of HMS *Ryde* off Omaha beach while acting as AA defence for the Mulberry Harbour, June 1940.

HMS *Ryde* as an anti-aircraft ship.

RYDE

1940 — 1945

WAR SERVICE

MINESWEEPER

FLAK SHIP

ESCORT VESSEL

NORMANDY INVASION

Commemorative plaque installed as a record of PS *Ryde*'s wartime career.

Richard Halton

1934.

H.M.S. "PRESIDENT"
H.M.S. "EFFINGHAM"
H.M.S. "SALADIN"
H.M.S. "GANGES"
H.M.S. "PEMBROKE"
H.M.S. "EGLINTON"
H.M.S. "VICTORY"
H.M.S. "KING ALFRED"
H.M.S. "EXCELLENT"
H.M.S. "LOCHINVAR"
H.M.S. "BOYNE"
H.M.S. "RYDE"
H.M.S. "EASTBOURNE"
H.M.S. "BLACKPOOL"
H.M.S. "MAENAD"
H.M.S. "GOZO"

1946.

Commemorative tankard detailing the naval service of Eric Gould.

Courtesy of his son, Gregory

As with most ships, PS *Ryde*'s appearance changed over the years. Certain marked physical differences provide a quick way to determine approximate dates for photographs. The images on these two pages highlight the main differences. The main deck saloon windows ahead of the bridge and a continuous deck house astern of the funnel are clear indicators that this is a pre-war image. Note that *Sandown* still had a continuous deckhouse after the war.

Graham Shaw Collection

Immediately after the war PS *Ryde* could be seen without the forward saloon windows and a gap in the after deckhouse. The radar on her foremast was added for the 1950 season.

Nigel Lawrence Collection

The main mast was added in 1954 to carry a second navigation light.

Nigel Lawrence Collection

The livery changed in 1965 to a British Rail scheme. Prior to that the livery had been basically the same as in Southern Railway days. PS *Sandown* and PS *Ryde* at Portsmouth.

John Goss LBIPP

In 1965/66 both masts were extended, raising the navigation lights.

John Goss LBIPP

When the ship was converted to a boatel in 1972 on the Isle of Wight the forward saloon windows were re-instated and the funnel livery changed to match *Medway Queen*.

John Hulse

PS *Ryde* leaving Clarence Pier in 1968.

John Hulse

PS *Ryde* going astern. Very obviously burning coal.

Barry J Eagles

The paddle steamers PS *Portsdown*, PS *Shanklin*, and PS *Merstone*, with PS *Whippingham* in reserve until she too was requisitioned, had remained on the ferry service in the Second World War. PS *Portsdown* and PS *Whippingham* were temporarily requisitioned for Operation Dynamo, the evacuation from Dunkirk and PS *Whippingham* was finally requisitioned for naval service in 1941.

PS *Portsdown* was sunk in the Solent by a mine early in the morning of 20th September 1941 with the loss of 23 lives; 15 of the 37 passengers and 8 of the crew of 11 including her captain, the local fleet's Senior Master, Captain H A Chandler.

This required temporary reassignment of PS *Solent* from the Lymington-Yarmouth service. The others had been requisitioned and converted for minesweeping, and all except *Southsea* survived the war and eventually returned to railway service. HMS *Southsea* was mined on 16th February 1941 as her flotilla passed the North Tyne Pier Light. The vessel was beached but declared a total loss. Eight officers and men were lost from the crew. In July 1945 PS *Sandown* and PS *Whippingham* had not yet returned from the Royal Navy and only PS *Merstone* and PS *Shanklin* were available, along with PS *Ryde*, for that first post-war summer season.

HMS *Ryde* was decommissioned and returned to civilian service. She was given what the company termed an austerity refit in Southampton in a very short time; around three months. She was returned to close to her pre-war outward condition; the most noticeable differences being a less rounded front to the bridge, fewer large main deck saloon windows forward of the bridge and a portion of the aft deckhouse (the first class smoking lounge) removed. On the 7th July 1945 she ceremoniously re-joined the fleet and made her initial crossing from Portsmouth Harbour Station to Ryde Pier. The event coincided with the introduction of the Southern Railway Company's new summer timetable. The *Isle of Wight County Press* commented that her return would be welcomed by the people of the island who had endured uncomfortably crowded conditions during "the emergency". The *County Press* also suggested that passengers used to wartime conditions would find little amiss in her condition and the facilities offered. They surmised that a vast improvement in the service could be expected.

PS *Ryde* was back in the Southern Railway livery of black and white hull, white superstructure and buff funnel. She flew the company house flag at the masthead and the red ensign astern. PS *Sandown* followed soon afterwards but PS *Whippingham* did not return to ferry duty until May 1946.

The directors of the Southern Railway celebrated the occasion with a cocktail party on board. The heads of island authorities and various public officials were invited and things were certainly cut fine on the schedule as it was reported that *"when the railway directors and officials arrived to take over at Southampton, the workmen engaged on the refit had only just completed their work"*. The mainland guests boarded in Portsmouth and the ship proceeded across the Solent to Ryde Pier where the Island guests came on board. They were greeted by Col. E Gore-Brown (Chairman of the Southern Railway), the Earl of Radnor (Vice Chairman), Lord Ebbisham GBE. (Director) and Sir Eustace Missenden (General Manager).

Refreshments were served in the saloon and Col. Gore-Browne acknowledged the difficulties experienced during the war and expressed admiration for the courtesy and efficiency of the staff during that time. He further remarked that *"it had been a really rush job to get her ready and all credit was due to the department responsible for her refit"*. Sir Godfrey Baring Bt. DL. (Chairman of the County Council) proposed a toast of *"success and long continuity of service of the Southern Railway"* although he also noted that *"if certain gentlemen were returned at the top of the poll in the election he expected the service would be taken over by the County Council"*. PS *Ryde* and her crew settled back into the routine of the ferry service, although it wasn't long before minor problems from the refit became apparent (as could be expected). Her capstan failed and she returned to the workshops for a replacement, re-joining the ferry service on 13th July.

Four piers were served by the ferries as they had been before the war although not all were available from the outset in 1945. Ryde Pier had continued in use throughout the war. Portsmouth Harbour station was badly damaged during the wartime air raids, although it continued in use, and it was repaired ready for post-war traffic when the expenditure of £37250 was authorised by the Board of Trade. Clarence Pier had also been damaged by air raids during the war and was not reopened until the 1950s. South Parade Pier was partly dismantled during the Second World War in an attempt to hinder any invasion attempt but was back in use by 1947.

Although the war was over, 1945 was not without excitements or problems for the ferry service. Many of the Southern Railway men were still serving in the armed forces so there were problems finding sufficient crews for the ferries. On weekdays it was only possible to run a third ship on one shift. On Saturdays 3 ships were run on double shifts with the crews working overtime. The fourth ship could not be used. Sundays saw 2 vessels working on double shifts. Passengers' luggage in advance also caused problems at weekends with over 800 items in trolley cages to be moved to or from the Isle of Wight. This problem was solved by hiring a suitable barge from Pickfords Ltd.

From Sunday 21st October 1945 the Isle of Wight and Solent were battered by a week of strong gale force winds with gusts up to 80mph and frequent squalls of torrential rain. Nearly 3 inches of rain were recorded for the period Sunday 21st to Friday 26th. Floating mines torn from their moorings by the waves were a very real threat and four were reported to have exploded on contact with rocks in Freshwater Bay. The *Isle of Wight Chronicle* advised that "naval experts will deal with any that come ashore but in the meantime people should keep off the beaches". Reports of damage to ships and property ashore were widespread. The ferry services were disrupted with delays in the morning and there were no sailings between Portsmouth and Ryde for a period in the afternoon of Thursday 25th. PS *Ryde*'s midday sailing was postponed. The wind was sufficiently strong to cause RMS *Queen Mary* to anchor and wait for an opportunity to enter Southampton Water.

In the evening of February 1st 1946 PS *Shanklin* suffered a boiler problem en-route to Ryde Pier. She turned back to Portsmouth and most passengers found accommodation for the night in the city. Some 50 or so remained at Harbour station and were allowed to stay on board PS *Ryde*. The ship's dynamos were kept running to provide heat and light and the passengers were taken to the Island on the first trip the next day.

On the 15th February 1946 PS *Ryde* collided with Spit Fort when on the early morning mail service. She left Ryde Pier at 5am but ran into thick fog. She was slowing down to drop anchor when she collided with the fort causing damage to her bows.

1947 turned out to be a busy year for the ferries. The five available steamers found it difficult to keep up with demand and long queues formed on Ryde pier on Saturdays. Fortunately the weather was mostly good although on one foggy morning the service could not start from Portsmouth until around 10am. The queue nearly reached the pier gates. Even on normal summer Saturdays the queue would run across the pier head and perhaps 50 yards back down the pier itself. If it was really busy that might be 100 yards, and there was no shelter if it rained. The queue reduced dramatically if one of the larger ships loaded but would build up again as the smaller vessels took their turn.

On 1st January 1948 the main railway companies, including the Southern Railway, were nationalised. The Southern Railway, including the ferries, became the Southern Region of British Railways. Like their predecessor British Railways would run special cruises or excursions from time to time to generate additional revenue and Southampton docks and the famous transatlantic liners were favourite subjects of these events. In July 1949, from Monday 25th to Friday 29th, they were advertising "Luxury Cruises" from Portsmouth Harbour on PS *Ryde* for a fare of three shillings. Three cruises each day, each of two hours duration. In the mornings it was Portsmouth Harbour and Spithead, in the afternoons and evenings Cowes and Calshot. These trips were in addition to regular cruises by PS *Whippingham* which for a fare of five shillings included the special attraction of seeing RMS *Queen Elizabeth*. On Monday and Tuesday the liner would be in dry dock and on Wednesday and Thursday in the Ocean Dock. On the Friday PS *Ryde*'s cruise included viewing RMS *Queen Elizabeth* at Spithead as she headed out across the sea to America.

Towards the end of the Second World War the Southern Railway Company had decided to supplement and eventually replace the existing coal burning paddle steamers on the Portsmouth - Ryde route with modern twin screw diesel powered vessels. The initial plan was to order the construction of two such vessels. These were to be identical ships, named MV *Southsea* and MV *Brading*, to be built by William Denny and Brothers of Dumbarton. The new ships would sail under the British Railways flag from their day of introduction. They were 200 feet long and 46 feet beam with a draught of seven feet. Their passenger capacity was 1135 for each ship and they were powered by twin Sulzer 8 diesel engines giving a service speed of 14.5 knots. Presumably a similar performance capability to the paddlers suited the route and made timetabling easier. Each ship had a crew of 33 people. They were launched on 11th March 1948 and went into service with British Railways. MV *Southsea* was the first to enter service, on 1st November 1948. MV *Brading* entered service on 2nd December 1948. The new ships were equipped with "Cossor" navigation radar, the first ships on the route to

A model of PS *Ryde*, made for a newly married couple in 1952 who travelled to the mainland for their honeymoon on her. The Captain signalled ahead and the ships in Portsmouth Harbour sounded their sirens to acknowledge the newlyweds.

Isle of Wight Heritage Service

carry this equipment. It soon proved its value in foggy conditions and in November 1949 it was announced that PS *Ryde* and PS *Sandown* were also to be fitted with the same equipment at a cost of £3500 per ship.

One of the existing paddle steamers, PS *Merstone*, was withdrawn in 1950 and scrapped in 1952. The increasing numbers of passengers led to an order for a third new ship, MV *Shanklin*, also built by William Denny and Brothers, designed to replace the paddle steamer of the same name. The new MV *Shanklin* was launched on 22nd February 1951 with the ceremony being performed by Mrs V M Barrington-Ward whose husband was a member of the British Railways executive. As a result of experience gained from building and operating the MV *Brading* and MV *Southsea*, MV *Shanklin* was slightly different from her sisters. Her funnel was taller and she had increased passenger deck space and raised lifeboats. MV *Shanklin* was a one class ship and with her introduction the other vessels were also changed to be single class. MV *Shanklin* had a passenger capacity of 1377 in summer and 1151 in winter. Her power and speed characteristics were virtually identical to her sisters but the power transmission was different with the engines connected directly to the propeller shafts and not through gearboxes and clutches. This led to reliability issues in later years. MV *Shanklin* was withdrawn from service some years before her elder sisters and was sold to the Firth of Clyde Steam Packet Co. in 1980, who operated her as MV *Prince Ivanhoe*.

The now redundant PS *Shanklin* was sold to Cosens & Co. of Weymouth in 1951 where she served for another ten years as PS *Monarch*. The motor vessels were far more economical and larger so they took over the regular ferry services, relegating the surviving paddle steamers to summer relief work and excursions. There was still a preponderance of routine voyages and activity which people rarely record but punctuated by highlights and accidents.

In the early 1950s passenger numbers on the ferry service increased markedly. On Saturday 29th July 1950 61526 passengers were carried between Portsmouth and Ryde and on Saturday 26th July 1952 an all-time record was set when 64290 passengers were carried; 35975 to Ryde and 28315 from the island. The previous record number carried was on 12th August 1939, when boats

operating from Portsmouth Harbour, South Parade Pier, and Clarence Pier carried 62297 passengers. The 1952 record was set with only five ships operating but they had the advantage of the new motor vessels. PS *Ryde* had been put out of action the previous day with a broken paddle shaft.

As the fleet assembled for the 1953 Spithead Coronation Naval Review PS *Ryde* ran a preview cruise from

Bridge telegraph.

John Goss LBIPP

37

PASSENGER SERVICE

SOUTHSEA CLARENCE PIER; SOUTH PARADE PIER

AND

RYDE PIER I.O.W.

SUMMER SEASON - 1962

(Weather and other circumstances permitting)

FROM SOUTHSEA   SATURDAYS, 9th JUNE TO 8th SEPTEMBER

		a.m.	a.m.	p.m.	p.m.	p.m.	p.m.	p.m.	p.m.
Clarence Pier	dep. ..	10.25	11.25	12.25	1.25	2.25	3.25	4A25	5A25
Ryde Pier	arr. ..	10.50	11.50	12.50	1.50	2.50	3.50	4A50	5A50

"A" runs 14th July to 11th August ONLY.

FROM RYDE

					p.m.	p.m.	p.m.
Ryde Pier	dep...	—	—	—	3.20	4.20	5.20
Clarence Pier	arr...	—	—	—	3.45	4.45	5.45

FROM SOUTHSEA   SUNDAYS, 10th JUNE TO 9th SEPTEMBER

		a.m.	p.m.	p.m.	p.m.	p.m.
Clarence Pier	dep. ..	10.30	12.15	2.25	4.10	5.30
South Parade Pier	dep. ..	10.55	—	2.50	—	—
Ryde Pier	arr. ..	11.20	12.40	3.15	4.35	5.55

FROM RYDE

		a.m.		p.m.	p.m.	p.m.
Ryde Pier	dep. ..	11.30	—	3.30	4.55	6.40
South Parade Pier	arr. ..	—	—	—	—	7.05
Clarence Pier	arr. ..	11.55	—	3.55	5.20	7.30

FROM SOUTHSEA   MONDAYS TO FRIDAYS, 11th JUNE TO 7th SEPTEMBER

		a.m.	a.m.	p.m.	p.m.	p.m.
Clarence Pier	dep. ..	9.50	11.50	2.20	4.10	5.30
South Parade Pier	dep. ..	10.15	11.30	2.45		
Ryde Pier	arr. ..	10.40	p.m. 12.15	3.10	4.35	5.55

FROM RYDE

		a.m.			p.m.	p.m.
Ryde Pier	dep. ..	10.55	—	—	4.55	6.40
South Parade Pier	arr. ..	11.20	—	—	—	7.05
Clarence Pier	arr. ..	11.45	—	—	5.20	7.30

PASSENGER FARES

	Ordinary	
Between	Single	Return
	s. d.	s. d.
Southsea and Ryde ...	3 3	6 6

LIGHT REFRESHMENTS OBTAINABLE IN FULLY LICENSED SALOONS

FOR PARTICULARS OF CRUISES PLEASE SEE SEPARATE HANDBILLS

Notice as to Conditions:—These tickets are issued subject to the Bye-Laws, Regulations and Conditions contained in the Publications and Notices of, or applicable to, the British Transport Commission.

All Services, Fares and Rates are liable to alteration without previous notice.

2685-30-1962   Holbrook & Son, Ltd., Printers, 154 Queen Street, Portsmouth

Summer Timetable 1962.

Graham Shaw Collection

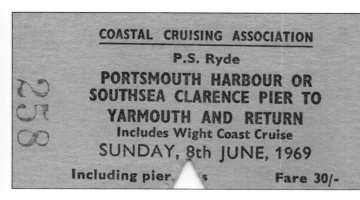

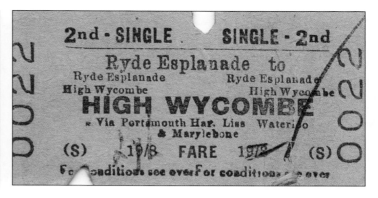

Portsmouth. John Hendy records that *"nearly 500 Eastbourne people who went to Portsmouth on Sunday 14th June for a preview of the Coronation review of the Fleet at Spithead, had the thrill of joining, at a distance, in the welcome to the Queen. Although the Russian cruiser Sverdlov was unable to accept an invitation to visit the town, the Eastbournians exchanged friendly waves with the Russian sailors. As the Ryde moved along the lines of ships, many of them preparing to dress over-all with flags, the tourists heard an interesting and entertaining running commentary from a naval friend of the British Railways official responsible for the organisation. Before berthing, the Ryde gave its passengers a close-up view of HMS Surprise, the ship from which the Queen was to review the Fleet next day."*

The 1953 Review of the Fleet at Spithead followed a similar pattern to the 1937 event, this time to celebrate the coronation of Her Majesty Queen Elizabeth II. As before large numbers of special trains were laid on to bring booked parties of visitors down from London and the ferries and many other vessels were booked to take those visitors round the fleet and in many cases to join the fleet being reviewed. PS *Ryde* and her fleet sisters were, of course, included in these arrangements.

Peter Seabroke remembers that *"In the summer of 1953 we went on a school trip (I was at school in Ryde) from Ryde pier on an excursion on PS Ryde around the fleet at the Spithead Review. The whole experience was fascinating and seemed to take all afternoon as there was a proper Navy in those days and of course there were ships from many other countries. Spent quite some time also looking at the engine. Unfortunately I did not have a camera in those days."*

The ratio of battleships to aircraft carriers had changed dramatically from the previous review in 1937 with HMS *Vanguard* being the sole Royal Navy representative of that type of warship. There were no less than nine British and Commonwealth aircraft carriers: HMS *Eagle*, HMS *Illustrious*, HMS *Implacable*, HMS *Indefatigable*, HMS *Indomitable*, HMCS *Magnificent*, HMS *Perseus*, HMAS *Sydney*, and HMS *Theseus*. The foreign navy representatives also did not include battleships, although some were still in service. Almost all vessels visiting were cruisers or destroyers.

The big day was Monday 15th June 1953 with ships arriving during the preceding days and special railway traffic scheduled for that Monday and for returns very early the following Tuesday. PS *Ryde*'s party appears to have been more locally based. PS *Ryde* took her place at the head of line "L" just off Ryde Pier. The schedule started at 8am with ships dressed overall. HMS *Surprise* acted as Royal Yacht since HMY *Britannia* was not yet complete and Her Majesty spent the morning receiving guests on board with luncheon

timed for 1pm. The remainder of the Royal Party arrived by train at 2.35 and HMS *Surprise* left the South Railway Jetty for Spithead at 3pm. She was preceded by the Trinity House vessel *Patricia* and escorted by HMS *Redpole* (a Black Swan class sloop). A royal salute was fired by the fleet as she approached. The review proper began at 3.30 with a fly-past of naval aircraft at 5.35. There were formal events on board HMS *Surprise* in the early evening and a formal dinner on board HMS *Vanguard* at 8.30. The fleet was illuminated at 10.30 and the firework display commenced at 10.40. Official celebrations were completed at midnight when the fleet illumination ended.

John Hendy also recorded a less happy incident from the Review when, on the 16th June, *"Scores of Review passengers on the British Transport Commission steamer Ryde staged a sit-down strike when the vessel returned to Portsmouth Harbour last evening (15th)"*. Apparently they were unhappy with the value for the £2 fare. According to the mooring plan, PS *Ryde* should have anchored northwest of Ryde Pier. A passenger stated that *"We were taken to a point west of the Spit Sand Port and saw little— only those with glasses could see anyone in the Surprise"*. She claimed that those ashore had a much better view. Many passengers refused to leave the ship. A British Railways official said that the bill advertised the trip as starting from Portsmouth Harbour to witness the Royal Naval Review.

In 1954 the regulations for navigation lights changed and it is likely that this is when a mainmast was added to the ship to carry a second light. In March of that year PS *Ryde* was in trouble again when she and her sister ship PS *Sandown* were in danger of drifting down onto HMY *Britannia* moored at the South Railway Jetty in Portsmouth Harbour. They were held off by four Portsmouth boatmen in two launches.

Although the full rebuild of Clarence Pier, including the amusement park, was not completed until June 1961 the cross-Solent ferry service to the island was reinstated on Monday 21st June 1954 after a lapse of 14 years. The next day, PS *Ryde* ran aground on a sandbank near Ryde. The small number of passengers on board were delayed for about an hour. Two days later, on 24th, PS *Ryde* went aground for the second time in 48 hours carrying passengers from Clarence Pier to Ryde. She was aground for more than an hour and a half and some passengers were taken off in the Gosport ferry, *Verda*, which carried them on to Ryde Pier. It was not until 11.40 that she was able to back off the shingle bank with her engines going full astern. She was found to be undamaged, and put back into immediate service but the whole embarrassing incident was witnessed by holiday makers and workers on the pier and by passengers on MV *Brading* and MV *Southsea*.

Easter 1954 was another record-breaker. Glorious

PS *Ryde* arriving at Ryde Pier 12-06-66.
John Goss LBIPP

weather throughout the weekend resulted in crowds more likely to be seen at the height of the summer. The passenger total for the Portsmouth - Ryde route was 42271 for the period Thursday to Tuesday with the highest number on Good Friday. There was a large number of cyclists attending a rally on the island and most of those were conveyed on PS *Ryde*. There were so many that when they returned on the Monday the two scheduled trips were not enough and PS *Ryde* made a third trip to bring them all back to the mainland.

On 30th June 1954, PS *Ryde* experienced mechanical difficulties and PS *Sandown* went to the rescue of her sister ship PS *Sandown* managed to secure a tow line and tow her to Portsmouth Harbour. On Tuesday 5th July 1955 the captain of PS *Ryde* spotted a dinghy in trouble as the ship was berthing at Ryde Pier. He raised the alarm and the yacht *White Adder*, which had been refuelling nearby, put out and rescued the two people clinging to the upturned dinghy. The dinghy and crew were returned safely to shore at the Rowing Club slipway.

Increasingly the paddlers were used for peak-time relief work, with the standard ferry service provided by the motor vessels. They were also used for excursions with Southampton Docks and the liners remaining a favourite destination. PS *Sandown* and PS *Ryde* were treated as interchangeable. When out of service, they were moored together alongside the coal hulk or a permanently anchored pontoon off Portsmouth Harbour station. On Sundays, the ship on the inside in the morning became the ship on the outside in the evening and they accordingly exchanged rosters for the following week.

The winter timetable operated for nine months of the year and provided an hourly service from Portsmouth Harbour to Ryde Pier on weekdays and a two hourly one on Sundays, leaving Portsmouth at 35 minutes past the hour and Ryde Pier at 30 minutes past, as governed by the London train timetable. It needed two motor ships to run the service. The third would be tied up in reserve or away having its winter overhaul. If one of the two operating the service broke down whilst the third was away, PS *Sandown* or PS *Ryde* would substitute as happened occasionally. Otherwise, the paddlers were out of service over winter, except that PS *Ryde* or PS *Sandown* would normally run a few relief services at Easter and the Whitsun Bank Holiday to avoid overcrowding.

The 1961 and 1962 summer timetables could theoretically be operated with four vessels. The 3 motor vessels were on a three week rota of 2 weeks on the Portsmouth Harbour – Ryde ferry followed by one on the Southsea – Ryde and Southampton Water/Docks cruises. For the timetabled half hourly Portsmouth Harbour to Ryde Pier service on Saturdays four vessels could not cope with the volume of traffic. Even with two extra vessels running, there were often very long queues as there had been in previous years. It was quite usual to see queues half way down Ryde Pier on Saturday mornings. People boarding the train at the Esplanade for the Pier Head frequently had to walk half way back down the pier towards the town!

During the rest of the week, one extra vessel was usually required in peak summer on sunny days to provide relief sailings and avoid day trippers having to wait too long. The schedule was, again, for an hourly service between Portsmouth Harbour and Ryde Pier from Sunday to Friday – not too different from the winter weekday service – and a half hourly service on Saturdays to try to move the hordes of people beginning or ending their holidays on the

Isle of Wight. The number of fast trains to and from London was increased from one to four per hour, some non-stop, and there were numerous Saturday only trains to and from other parts of the UK.

There was also a one ship service from Sunday to Friday from South Parade and Clarence Piers to Ryde Pier. On Saturdays, there was an advertised service from Clarence Pier to Ryde Pier but it was actually covered by the diesels on the Portsmouth Harbour run making additional calls.

Graham Shaw notes *"a bit more excitement"* on Thursday 7th September 1961: *"I went to get the 1610 sailing from Clarence Pier, which should have been taken by PS Ryde, to find PS Sandown waiting for me and no sign of PS Ryde anywhere. When I got to Ryde Pier, I saw MV Southsea, which should have been on the Southampton Docks cruise, travelling towards Southampton empty and at half speed (with engine trouble, it later transpired). Much later, having returned to Clarence Pier on PS Sandown, I saw PS Ryde appear from the direction of Southampton, with a good crowd on board and making a memorable pall of black smoke. She had presumably replaced MV Southsea on the cruise at short notice and was making a gallant effort to recover time."*

PS *Ryde* collided with Ryde Pier on Tuesday 25th July 1962. Her anchor caught and cracked a wooden pile and three fenders and other parts of the pier were damaged putting berth number two out of action for a few days. The paddler was only slightly dented. Another accident in 1963

saw PS *Ryde* towed back into Portsmouth by MV *Shanklin* when a rope fouled one of the paddle wheels.

The paddlers were in good condition and capable of creditable performances. Graham Shaw timed some of the runs and made the following notes: *"PS Ryde too was in excellent form and I recorded an astonishing 52 revs per minute on one trip from Clarence Pier to Ryde Pier – unfortunately she was seriously impeded by small yachts so the timing was no better than the 25 minute schedule. PS Sandown was reliable enough but painfully slow. Ryde was always notable for the amount of smoke it produced – far more than its quasi-sister Sandown (or Whippingham). Whippingham was faster than Ryde."*

"I only bought one weekly season ticket in 1962, finishing on Saturday 25th August, when I went on PS Whippingham seven times and Ryde once. PS Whippingham's first sailing had only 121 passengers as the first fast train from London was late – there could be no question of waiting for it because of the queues already building up at Ryde Pier – and reached Ryde Pier in 29 minutes. Later on a honeymoon couple were seen off on PS Whippingham at Ryde Pier by loudspeaker announcements and the foghorns of Whippingham and Ryde."

PS *Whippingham* was withdrawn at the end of the 1962 season and advertised for sale on 24th December as a day passenger paddle steamer capable of 15 knots on 1.7 tons of coal per hour. She left under tow for a Belgian firm of shipbreakers at 1700 on Friday 17th May 1963. The ship's

British Rail

Shipping Services

Sunday - 30th May 1965

SPECIAL CRUISE IN SOLENT BY THE PADDLE STEAMER 'RYDE' OR 'SANDOWN'

(Weather and other circumstances permitting)

PORTSMOUTH HARBOUR depart: 2.00 p.m. arrive back (approx.) 5.00 p.m.
RYDE PIER   depart: 2.35 p.m. arrive back (approx.) 5.35 p.m.

FARE FIVE SHILLINGS

Children under fourteen years - half fare

LIGHT REFRESHMENTS OBTAINABLE IN FULLY LICENSED SALOONS

As numbers embarked will be strictly limited, to avoid disappointment it is recommended that tickets be purchased in advance. (Priority will be given to members of the Paddle Steamer Preservation Society).

Notice as to Conditions: These tickets are issued subject to the Bye-laws, Regulations and Conditions contained in the Publications and Notices of, or applicable to, the British Railways Board

SER 7/1—2739—5   Holbrook & Son Ltd., Norway Road, Hilsea, Portsmouth

Solent Cruise advertisement.

Graham Shaw Collection

Grand Cruise through the Solent

to

SOUTHAMPTON DOCKS

by the British Rail Steamer

P.S. "RYDE"

on

Sunday, 7th September, 1969

TIMES

Dep. 13.45	PORTSMOUTH Harbour		arr. 18.30
Dep. 14.00	SOUTHSEA Clarence Pier		arr. 18.15
Dep. 14.15	SOUTHSEA South Parade Pier		*
Dep. 14.45	RYDE Pierhead		arr. 17.45

* Passengers disembark at Clarence Pier

FARES

From Portsmouth/Southsea 13/6
From Ryde 12/-

Children under 14 half fare
Special Rates for Parties of 10 or over
ADVANCE BOOKING ADVISED
Fares refunded if sailing cancelled

TEAS & LIGHT REFRESHMENTS AVAILABLE.
LICENSED BAR OPEN THROUGHOUT TRIP
AMPLE COVERED ACCOMMODATION

Cruise arranged with the kind co-operation of British Rail Shipping Division and subject to the Byelaws, Regulations and Conditions applicable to vessels of B.R. Board. Voyage subject to weather and circumstances permitting.

See overleaf for further details

Southampton Docks Cruise 1969.

Graham Shaw Collection

withdrawal seems to have been due to running costs. She had reputedly cost £39000 to get her into service in 1962 for just 6 days of use. The price for 1963 would have been £50000.

In 1963 the summer service was operated by the remaining five ships. Passenger numbers were declining, as they were at holiday destinations throughout the UK, due to decreased air fares and increased car use. The five ship fleet could cope and both PS *Ryde* and PS *Sandown* continued in service despite the costs of replacing expired hull plates in the winter overhauls. An alternative that was considered was to purchase a fourth motor ship which would probably have led to earlier withdrawal of at least one of the paddlers if it had happened.

Mick Watts has some recollections of PS *Ryde* from the early to mid-sixties when he was about 14 years old: *"My cousin was very much into fishing from Ryde Pier Head at the time and he had built his own fishing rod using the fairly newly available tapered fibreglass. All the parts you needed for this could be bought from Don's sports shop at the end of Cross Street, Ryde. Seeing his new rod, I decided to have a go at fishing but fibre glass was expensive for a try-out rod. Somehow I found myself in possession of a tapered steel tubular alternative which was an ex-wartime Army surplus jeep aerial, but how I came to have it I don't remember. Anyway, we soon found ourselves in Don's sports shop, buying eyes and ferrules, cork sections for the handle, reel fitting and a cheap reel. Many hours were then spent whipping the eyes onto the tube and assembling all the parts into a wonderful new fishing rod."*

"Desperate to try my new rod, we quickly organised a fishing trip to Ryde Pier Head. In those days you could fish anywhere on the Pier as long as you kept away from the ferry berthing area. The day we chose to fish was in the summer when the diesel ships MV Brading, MV Shanklin and MV Southsea were the regular ferries bringing thousands of holidaymakers to the Island. The Ryde was then brought back into service to give additional capacity for the peak periods. With our lines cast we knew we were well away from the diesel ferries path and there were no problems. Later in the morning we saw the Ryde approaching. Staring at this not too common sight, I failed to appreciate that she was taking a more direct path to the berth. As she passed us, my new fishing rod disappeared from its stand at an impressive velocity as the line wrapped itself around the paddle wheel. With a feeble splash my new rod disappeared beneath the blue summer waves to be gone forever. I was devastated! I completed the day's fishing with my cousin's hand line but with no success, just went home with an empty fishing rod bag!"

Graham Shaw noted that *"An innovation in 1964 was that PS Ryde ran two advertised cruises from Portsmouth Harbour and Ryde Pier to Southampton Water (actually advertised to be undertaken by Ryde or Sandown and with the statement that "Priority will be given to members of the Paddle Steamer Preservation Society"). These took place on Whit Sunday and Sunday 14th June, the fare being a very reasonable five shillings (25p), less than the usual diesel fare. They were pretty successful, with over 600 passengers being carried on the first of them, surely enough to compensate for the additional fuel costs? In those days, enthusiasts were still incurably optimistic and we started dreaming of a more extensive cruising programme and even converting one of the paddlers to oil firing. In the real world, in 1965, just one similar cruise was run by Ryde, on Whit Sunday, quite successful despite the weather, but that was our lot."*

In 1965 PS *Ryde* and PS *Sandown* were reported in the new British Rail colours of blue hull, white upper-works. This was topped by a red funnel with the British Rail "double arrow". For maritime use this symbol was slightly modified so that the upper arrow faced forward on both sides of the funnel. During the winter of 1965/66 both masts were extended, presumably to raise the height of the navigation lights.

British Rail's Divisional Shipping Manager, Mr L H R Wheeler, described the improvements made to the ferry service for 1966/7. The new hydraulic gangways and planned modifications to the motor vessels had drastically cut turn round times and queueing. The motor vessels would be able to each carry 1300 passengers. The Portsmouth service could now be operated by three vessels allowing them to release PS *Sandown* which was withdrawn and sold. PS *Ryde* would be used to relieve

Cruise ticket.

Graham Shaw Collection

congestion and continue to operate the service from the Southsea piers. Finally the "new" electric trains would operate on the Isle of Wight and parcels were being packaged in containers at Fratton before shipment to reduce handling. In reality the "new" trains were refurbished London Transport underground stock. It was also intended that parcels services in the opposite direction would be offered and businesses on the Island could pack containers on their premises. Together, these measures meant there were no paddle steamer cruises in that year. Saturdays remained busy but passenger numbers continued to decline on the ships although not on the hovercraft service.

In 1968 PS *Ryde* ran a special cruise to meet Alec Rose as he returned from his round the world voyage in the

Assistance from MV *Shanklin* after the mishap with a rope in 1963.

Portsmouth History Centre

yacht; *Lively Lady*. Later that same year, from 11th to 15th September, she was hired out to Gilbey's Gin and ran excursions on the Thames to promote their product. One of the trips was captured in a short film by British Pathe and is available to watch online. Loading at Tower Pier we see passengers enjoying their first drinks while down below the stoker is busy preparing the fire for the trip and ensuring there is a full head of steam. The "Gin Flag" is hoisted to the masthead and the ship casts off, turning in the Pool of London and heading past the Tower and through Tower Bridge which opens to let her pass. Pearly Kings and Queens tuck in to the traditional jellied eels washed down with gin as they head downstream past the Italian training ship Amerigo Vespucci anchored in the river and on past the Cutty Sark and Greenwich. After shots of the engines running and more stoking of the coal fired boilers the film cuts to views of the on-board casino and a ball, organised by the RNLI, on their way back to Tower Pier.

Press cuttings from the time also record a reunion of HMS *Ryde*'s wartime crew attended by around 30 members. On this occasion PS *Ryde* was commanded by Captain E L Yelland and they sailed from Tower Pier to Greenwich. Among them was Donald Beamer who had commanded HMS *Ryde* during Operation Overlord. The silver band on board played *Rule Britannia* as they watched PS *Ryde* berth at Tower Pier. The veterans were then piped aboard. The press report also mentions Mr A J Budden who was the ship's Chief Engineer when she was minesweeping off the East Coast. He had also served as engineer on board before the war. Despite the distraction of bands, cheering crowds on the river bank and even lunch, Mr. Budden apparently remained in the engine room for almost the whole trip.

PS *Ryde* continued as relief vessel on the main Portsmouth Harbour to Ryde Pier route in 1969. She was given a winter overhaul during 1968/9 so as to maintain her reliability in service at a cost of about £15000. Immediately after her return, in May 1969, PS *Ryde* stood in for a few days on the Portsmouth Harbour service when MV *Shanklin* and MV *Southsea* performed cruises around the NATO Review fleet. Derek Gawn recorded her on ferry sailings in both May and June and on one occasion in July.

She sailed on a small number of excursions in 1969, mostly aimed at the paddle steamer enthusiast market. There was an afternoon cruise on 1st June from all three Portsmouth/Southsea piers to Cowes (non-landing) and around the Naval Dockyard. On Sunday 8th June PS *Kingswear Castle* was reported cruising off the Beaulieu River where she met up with the Coastal Cruising Association's chartered trip on PS *Ryde*. Graham Shaw was on PS *Ryde* that day: "The cruise was very well loaded. But Ryde had to make a 50 minute stop at Royal Pier Southampton to allow passengers to get some lunch as her catering facilities were too primitive for a full day cruise – if you booked in advance, you could eat at the Mecca Restaurant. It was particularly gratifying later in the day to pass PS Kingswear Castle, acquired by PSPS in 1967, on a trial trip to Buckler's Hard. Again, a tribute is in order to the two stokers who were on duty for 13 hours, at least 9 of them underway."

The PS *Kingswear Castle* cruise carried the Ridett family (owners of the *Medway Queen* Club and later to purchase PS *Ryde*) and friends from the Isle of Wight to the Beaulieu river. Many of them were dressed in Edwardian costume. The two paddle steamers were filmed from the air by the

PS *Ryde*'s post-war ship's bell.

Richard Halton

BBC for a programme *"Beside the Seaside"* in the *"Bird's Eye View"* series narrated by John Betjeman. This can be found on BBC IPlayer.

The *Isle of Wight County Press* reported on 23rd August 1969 that the last cruise of PS *Ryde* would be on 7th September, chartered to the PSPS. She was expected to be withdrawn at end of the season as a replacement motor vessel was delivered in June. The cruise was jointly organised with the Isle of Wight Steam Railway and both organisations took the opportunity to raise funds.

Peter Seabroke also remembered that *"I went with my Father on the last excursion (organised by the Paddle Steamer Preservation Society) in the Solent. The PS Ryde came across from Portsmouth, picked up more passengers, including us, from Ryde Pier and went on down the Solent to Southampton Water and then up nearly as far as the Ocean Terminal and back. This was September 1969. During the trip some of us had a tour of the area down below the engine crankshaft. Had a chat with the Engineer who had previously worked for J. S. White. Two or three people at a time went down into the stokehold and chatted*

Captain Eric Yelland, PS *Ryde*'s final master 10-08-69.

John Hendy

PS *Ryde* departing
Ryde Pier 08-06-68.
John Goss LBIPP

to the Stoker (a Scotsman). It was very hot down there! I remember being fascinated to see how all the auxiliaries were directly powered by steam; the generator, the capstans and the steering motors. At that time she was in very good condition and everyone was hoping that she could be kept in commission."

Derek Gawn recorded PS *Ryde* in service for the last time on 13th September: *"She took over the service from 3pm and worked (with MV Brading on the opposite turn):*

3.40pm Portsmouth to Ryde
4.30pm Ryde to Portsmouth
5.40pm Portsmouth to Ryde
6.30pm Ryde to Portsmouth
7.40pm Portsmouth to Ryde
8.30pm Ryde to Portsmouth (and finish)

We sailed on PS Ryde from 4.30 at Ryde until 8.10pm at Ryde. We then watched her leave – dark by then – at 8.30pm on her very final sailing (she sounded 3 long blasts) MV Southsea & MV Shanklin were both on late night charters".

At the end of 1969 PS *Ryde* would have needed extensive re-plating of the hull if she were to continue in service, a common reason for withdrawing old paddle steamers, and In February 1970 she was offered for sale at around £10000. A number of offers were received and Portsmouth City Council started investigating the possibility of PS *Ryde* being preserved in a new transport and industrial museum at Eastney. Suddenly the old ship became newsworthy with many letters, editorials and articles in the local paper. It was reported that the Victoria and Albert Museum was considering a grant and the Duke of Edinburgh, as President of the Maritime Trust, and the Duke of Westminster, as its Chairman, were *"thoroughly appreciative"* of the enterprise being shown by the City

Council.

The local press carried correspondence both for and against this proposal and one notable letter contained the suggestion *"that if the Parks Department spent less on roses to obstruct motorists' views at roundabouts the money would surely be there".* Eventually, Portsmouth City Council approved the purchase of a temporary berth for PS *Ryde* in Langstone Harbour, pending the opening of the new museum and a councillor bid £11000 to secure her for the City. In the event, PS *Ryde* was towed out of Portsmouth Harbour on 16th September 1970, having been sold to Alan Ridett for use as a restaurant and accommodation ship at the Medway Queen Marina, Binfield, Isle of Wight,

Footnote:

British Rail granted custody of PS *Ryde*'s bell and war service plaque to the Sea Cadet Corps. A ceremony was held on board MV *Brading* on Sunday 29th November 1970. The ceremony took place in heavy rain on the mid-ships shelter deck; it had been arranged by Alderman Mark Woodnutt who was also present along with British Rail officials. Some of HMS *Ryde*'s wartime crew were also there. The presentation was made by Mrs. Wheeler, wife of Captain L H R Wheeler (British Rail Shipping Services Manager, Portsmouth) with the addition of a framed colour photograph of PS *Ryde*; a personal gift from Captain Wheeler. Lieutenant Hickman, commanding officer of the Sea Cadet unit thanked Captain Wheeler and the Marine Services of British Rail. The guests were taken on a short cruise on the Solent and the cadets were invited to the bridge where the ship's master, Captain B Bowers, and mate, J N Bligh, explained the working of the ship's instruments.

PS *Ryde* at
Southsea Clarence
Pier.
John Goss LBIPP

PS *Ryde* at the
coaling hulk, PS
Sandown beyond.
Author's collection

Three views of PS *Ryde* at Newhaven during winter lay-up and maintenance periods:

A freshly repainted PS *Ryde* at Newhaven.
OurNewhaven website - Derek Longly

Mr. Bob Holden working on the radar.
OurNewhaven website - Colin Holden

PS *Ryde* on the maintenance grid at Newhaven 07-03-69.
John Hendy

PS *Ryde*, as the Gin Palace approaching Tower Pier 13-09-68.

Fraser G. MacHaffie

PS *Ryde* leaving Tower Pier on hire to Gilbey's Gin in 1968.

PSPS Collection

PS *Ryde* at London Tower Pier.

John Goss LBIPP

John Hendy remembers a voyage on PS *Ryde* from Newhaven, where she had been for her winter overhaul and lay-up, to Portsmouth for the 1968 summer season:

"Prior to the commencement of her penultimate season in service, on 20th May 1968 I was fortunate enough to join a party of 12 members of the Coastal Cruising Association for the Ryde's delivery voyage to Portsmouth. It was a grey and rather miserable day and the planned morning departure was postponed due to a lack of water in the river. Fortunately the afternoon high tide was more promising and after finalising the paperwork, the group made its way on board. The Dover-based car ferry Normannia was berthed immediately ahead of us, still in her winter hibernation, as we slowly made our way down the River Ouse past the Dieppe service ferry Falaise and towards the inviting English Channel. Once outside the harbour, the ship dropped the pilot and swung through 360 degrees in order to adjust her compass. In those days before the advent of Global Positioning Systems, a line was attached astern in order to measure the distance travelled and every so often, an AB would be despatched from the wheelhouse to check on our progress.

The Ryde's interior accommodation seemed eerily empty and typically dark. On a 30 minute service crossing to Ryde it was sometimes difficult to explore her but the opportunity of an approximate 65-mile sail in an all but empty ship allowed one to feel that she had been well and truly scrutinised. The Southern Railway and its successor, British Railways, had never really appreciated that in a changing age, passengers might well appreciate a degree of comfort

on such a brief crossing although in recent years they had successfully modified and updated the facilities on the three diesel ferries which operated the year-round service.

In truth, the journey along the Sussex coast to Portsmouth is not the most picturesque of coastal cruises and the Ryde was steered well off shore. Once the chalk cliffs between Peacehaven and Rottingdean had been passed, there began the long urban sprawl of Brighton, Hove, Shoreham, Worthing and beyond. Eventually rounding Selsey Bill, the eastern end of the Isle of Wight came into view and, as the ship entered Spithead, in the distance we caught sight of the prototype SRN-4 hovercraft which was engaged on trials from her builders at East Cowes. Plodding ever westwards in a coal-fired paddle steamer, it proved to be a remarkable contrast with what was then perceived to be the cutting edge technology of the day. But, just like the paddle steamers, cross-Channel hovercraft are now consigned to history. The sun finally broke through the gloom as we entered Portsmouth Harbour. The Isle of Wight passenger ferry MV Brading was alongside the station while half-sister MV Shanklin occupied the inner berth of what is now termed the 'odds & evens' (mooring pontoon). The Ryde sailed past before back-paddling onto her berth. However, not having been used since the previous September, her mooring ropes were as dry as dust and several efforts to throw the lines failed as they were caught in the breeze. Leaning over the starboard bridge wing, the Captain advised that the ropes should be wetted prior to being thrown and, following his wise advice, very soon we were alongside and secure."

Text and pictures by John Hendy

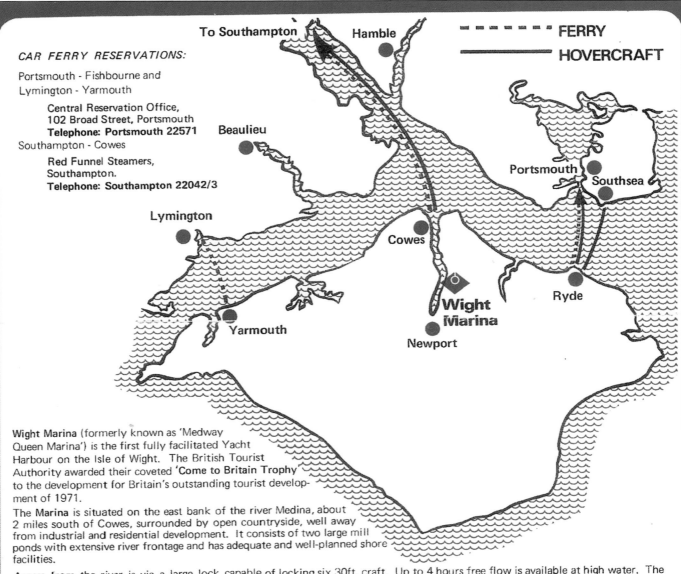

- - - - - - - **FERRY**
——————— **HOVERCRAFT**

Wight Marina (formerly known as 'Medway
Queen Marina') is the first fully facilitated Yacht
Harbour on the Isle of Wight. The British Tourist
Authority awarded their coveted **'Come to Britain Trophy'**
to the development for Britain's outstanding tourist develop-
ment of 1971.

The **Marina** is situated on the east bank of the river Medina, about
2 miles south of Cowes, surrounded by open countryside, well away
from industrial and residential development. It consists of two large mill
ponds with extensive river frontage and has adequate and well-planned shore
facilities.

Access from the river is via a large lock capable of locking six 30ft. craft. Up to 4 hours free flow is available at high water. The
dredged channel depth ranges from 3ft. at low water spring tides to 15ft. at high water. The site is linked by surfaced drive to the
main Ryde/Newport road where public transport is available to all parts of the Island. Mainland Yachtsmen wishing to keep their
craft in the Marina will be provided with transport which will run from Cowes to the site during weekends, linking up with the
Hovercraft and Red Funnel Steamer Services.

EAST MEDINA MILL.
Nr COWES.
NEWPORT. ISLE OF WIGHT.
Telephone: NEWPORT 4751.

Wight Marina brochure of 1973.

East Cowes Heritage Centre

A publicity photograph for the marina found behind panelling during the repair programme.

Dave Cannon Collection

In the mid-1960s a group of businessmen from the Isle of Wight led by Alan Ridett with his cousin Colin Ridett and Robert Trapp took over the lease of the land that was to become the Medway Queen Marina. The marina was built on the site of a tide mill, the East Medina Mill, which had been built in 1790 by William Porter of Newport. By 1965 the mill had long gone and the site was disused. Plans for the marina's first phase gained approval in March 1966. The original marina prospectus clearly shows a great number of proposed moorings for boats in the mill pond and river. Those in the river would be tidal. Phase one was for 130 berths with 6ft of water at all times, controlled by an access lock. The lock gates were constructed of Greenheart, one of the hardest woods available and came from an old pier on the island. The lock gates ran on old tank wheels and still do today. The non-tidal berths were in the large mill pond, *Medway Queen*, and later *Ryde Queen*, being moored in the small pond. Mud berths were also provided on the foreshore with a slipway and hard standing available.

They purchased the veteran paddle steamer *Medway Queen* from the breakers for £6000 in 1965 for use as a clubhouse, restaurant and nightclub and when the ship arrived it was reported as being berthed at East Medina Mill. She was re-furbished for her new role and opened as The *Medway Queen* Club on 14th May 1966. The opening ceremony was performed by John Graves who had been First Lieutenant of HMS *Medway Queen* during the Dunkirk

evacuation in 1940 and who had maintained links with the ship ever since.

Moorings were advertised at the *Medway Queen* Marina in May 1966 at the same time as the *Medway Queen* Club opened. The club and marina were run together and were obviously complementary as boat owners could eat and drink in the club if they so wished. Alan Ridett told the *Isle of Wight County Press* that *Medway Queen* would be kept afloat in the smaller mill pond, although it was not flooded at that time, and that the larger pond would provide 50 individual deep water berths for the marina. This would be the first phase of the marina's development. There were 50 mud berths currently available. The site was planned to be landscaped and the club had some 400 members at the time of opening. Mr. Ridett welcomed the guests and thanked them for their role in saving the ship from the breakers. He also thanked all who had made personal donations to the cause. He welcomed the first members of the *Medway Queen* Club who would be the lifeblood of the ship from then on and paid tribute to the round the clock efforts of staff and friends to get everything ready.

The club thrived and quickly outgrew the accommodation provided by the old ship so, in 1970, Alan Ridett purchased PS *Ryde*, from British Rail. Alan and his son, Mark went to Portsmouth Harbour to meet a British Rail manager. They handed over a cheque for £12000 which was apparently the scrap value of the ship. She was towed to the marina on Wednesday 16th September of that year under the

Work on the marina development in the early 1970s - earthworks.
Mark Ridett

The foundations in course of construction. Note the PS *Kingswear Castle* in the background.
Mark Ridett

One of the heavy earthmovers used on the marina and to position the ships. *Medway Queen* on the left, PS *Ryde* still moored in the background.
Roger Caws

PS *Ryde* under tow on her way to the marina in 1970.

Mark Ridett

Moored in the river awaiting positioning, watched by Chris Tebbutt and his mother.

Bob Tebbutt, courtesy of Chris Tebbutt

Ryde Queen conversion in 1972.

Barry J Finch

supervision of the Cowes yacht rigger Harry Spencer. PS *Ryde* was not moved to her final position immediately as development of the marina was continuing. The access road was often muddy in the winter; at one time taxis refused to go down the road and young ladies in high heels covered in mud had to walk to the ships!

After the marina was developed things improved but at one stage when it got extremely foggy several cars actually drove into the marina by mistake. No one drowned and concrete flower boxes were built along the edge to prevent this from happening again, before someone did drown. The lagoon and car park at Island Harbour were largely built up with stone deposited by the demolition contractor Tregar & Sons of Gosport from the former Royal National Hospital at Ventnor. The mill pond dredging was carried out by two RB22 drag bucket excavators and the marina was considered to be ready for a formal opening on Friday 28th May 1971. The ceremony was performed by M. Claude Prouvoyeur, the Mayor of Dunkirk although PS *Ryde* was still not in use. This event was, again, attended by John Graves and his family.

Two heavy tracked earthmovers were also being used in the development work and their tasks included moving *Medway Queen* from her original berth to a new one in November 1971 and then pulling PS *Ryde* in from her position in the mill pond to her new permanent mooring position. This was done in the middle of the night, during a very high tide. Mark Ridett remembers that several steel cables snapped under the immense strain when she touched the bottom. PS *Ryde* was opened for a Spectacular Pre-refit Evening on Friday January 7th 1972. During that month 1000 lifejackets and 30 tons of welsh

steam coal were offered for sale to the public through small ads in the local press. Lifejackets were 50p each and the coal 75p per hundredweight (about 51 kilograms). The marina name was changed to Wight Marina in 1972 and the ship became *Ryde Queen*. The first newspaper reference to the new name, Wight Marina, was in April of that year.

The *Ryde Queen* was advertised as Open to Visitors from the Bank Holiday on Monday, 29th May 1972 and a formal opening of the renamed *Ryde Queen* as a boatel took place at 2pm on Wednesday June 14th with a tea dance on the aft upper deck at 4pm to the music of the Paddle Boat Shufflers. The restaurant was open for dinner between 7pm and 1am the following day and an Opening Night Gala Dance was held with live music and a stereo disco from 8pm to 1am. The ceremony was performed by Miss Wight Marina. Mark Ridett and Quentin Reynolds (one time manager) remember that she was Carolyn Moore, Miss Great Britain in 1971, and they made a new sash with Miss Wight Marina on it for the opening. She was the girlfriend of footballer George Best and stayed with the Ridetts. Mark remembers that she spent a lot of preparation time in the bathroom and that she obtained a signed photograph of George Best for him and his brother.

The conversion drawings show the cabin layout for the boatel operation. There were five double berth cabins and 2 larger suites on the main deck and 6 doubles and two singles on the lower deck. Toilets etc. were provided on both decks and there were shower rooms below. The reception area was on the main deck and there was a galley and snack bar in the port sponson. The main entrance was through the existing aft access on the starboard sponson, with new doors fitted, and a fire escape

Two views on board PS *Ryde* during her conversion to a boatel and club in 1972.
Both: Barry J Finch

The Ryde Queen Boatel in its heyday.

Medway Queen (left) and *Ryde Queen* in their new positions in the marina.

with a gangway was added through a new opening at the forward end of the ship. A staff entrance was provided at the forward end of the sponson. The engine room alleyways were fitted with fire doors.

The ship's engine was left in situ as a visitor attraction. Forward of the engine room the large main restaurant was on the main deck. The saloon windows that were lost in the wartime and post-war conversions were reinstated and the two forward hatches were replaced with large skylights over the restaurant. The main deck had the Funnel Bar with a purpose built dance floor where the boiler had been. This compartment had originally spanned both lower and main decks to accommodate a boiler. Here the Eric Stevens Trio played (they had also played on the *Medway Queen* for years). In the Funnel Bar the original funnel was turned into a feature and enclosed with a glass top enabling visitors to watch the night sky from within. On the lower deck was the Boiler Room Bar and Disco with a new access stairway from the main deck. This bar extended from the original boiler room through to the bow where there was another stairway leading back up to the main deck and fire escape. The drawings show that bulkheads forward of the boiler, either side of the bunkers, were removed and additional supports put in to maintain the structure of the ship. Dave Allington was the Resident DJ here and he too also worked on the *Medway Queen*. The lower bar was also referred to as Keel Bar at times. An awning was added to the aft portion of the promenade deck to provide an additional music and dance venue – at least in summer.

Advertisements from 1972 state that "*the Ryde Queen Boatel will be open for the season and throughout the year*". She is described as having "*an upper deck with a panoramic view of the marina and river, and a stroll along the boat decks will bring you to the quarter-deck dance floor, which is fully enclosed with awning and side screens. There you will find dancing to live music seven nights a week and on sunny afternoons there will be entertainments Paddle Boat Shuffle Style. The companionways on the main decks, with their view of the original engines, lead to the luxuriously appointed restaurant which seats 100 people. Below on the lower deck is the Boiler Lounge Bar, with a maple dance floor and the Island's latest stereo discotheque, which will also open seven nights a week.*"

Advertisements also mention the Funnel Bar and, in 1973 only, the Keel Bar. The *Ryde Queen* took over the more up-market activities from *Medway Queen*, which reopened as a disco after her own refit during the autumn/winter of

1972/3. The restaurant and private event functions such as wedding receptions moved to the new ship. The two ships and the marina services were advertised jointly in the local press and for some years the combined businesses appeared to thrive. But although the ships were very successful the business as a whole struggled. Alan Ridett (who was an architect) realised that the key to the success of the place was to build residential properties on the site, as has now happened, but in those days the Medina Valley was sacrosanct and the planners would not let any

Invitation to the opening of the "Ryde Queen Boatel".
Courtesy of Mrs Jenni Le Mouton

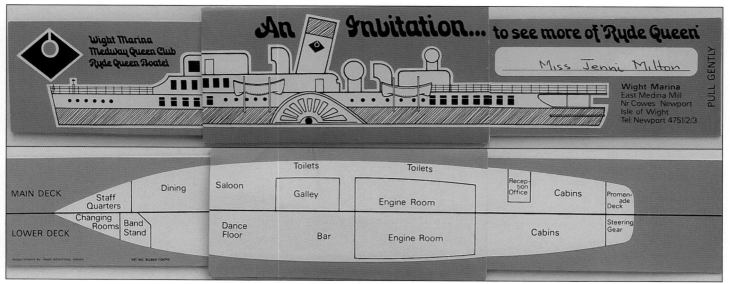

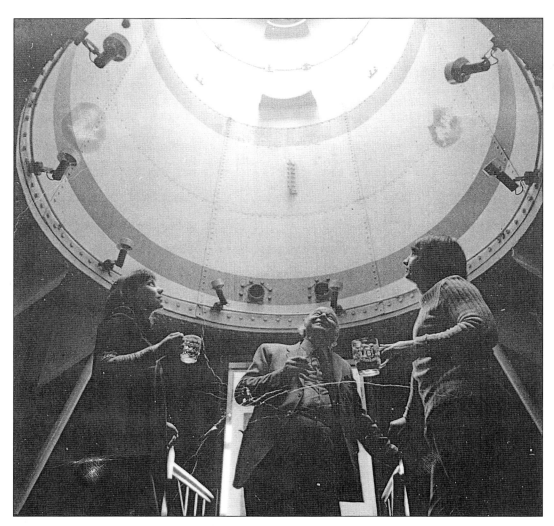

Publicity shots for the *Ryde Queen*.

The Funnel Bar with the glass cap in place on the funnel.

The main restaurant in what had been the forward saloon. Note the skylights installed in place of the baggage hatches.

Both: Courtesy of Quentin Reynolds

DJ Dave Allington who performed on both *Medway Queen* and *Ryde Queen*.

Courtesy of Quentin Reynolds

Alan Ridett and his wife, Anne who brought *Ryde Queen* to the Island.

Mark Ridett Collection

properties be built. Dave Cannon was another regular DJ on the *Ryde Queen* and *Medway Queen*. The *Ryde Queen* was his favourite venue, because not only was he a DJ there but did the maintenance as well. He could be painting it during the day, and playing records in it at night.

An October 1972 advertisement stresses the restaurant facilities for business lunches and includes the Paddle Steamer Steak Bar. Bookings for private functions could be taken. The Funnel Bar served lunchtime snacks and evening discos in the Boiler Bar featured Dave Allington's disco and the Ryde Queen Go-Go Girls. The evening admission charge was 30p. In December the Miss Wight Marina competition was advertised with live music from Pseudo-Foot. The band names changed from time to time but often musicians from one would turn up in its successor or would be part of two groups playing on different evenings. There was a dress code of "Conventional attire – no jeans! No T-shirts!" Over the Christmas period the ship offered a full programme with a dinner dance on Wednesday 20th December, lunch with entertainment from the Eric Stevens Trio on Christmas Eve (Sunday) and a traditional Christmas Lunch at £2.75 per head on Christmas Day. On Boxing Day there was a coffee and sherry morning with a running buffet at £1.25 per head from 1pm onwards. There was also a New Year's Eve dinner dance.

The *Medway Queen* and *Ryde Queen* in their heyday had a thousand people on them every Friday and Saturday night. Newport's pubs, and pubs in other towns on the Island, emptied out at 10pm as everybody headed to the two ships (pubs closed at 11pm anyway) and the income from the ships helped to finance the marina development.

Very early in 1973 a promotional event held on the shore near *Ryde Queen* was the Tunnel of Fire world record attempt by Dick Sheppard. The original announcement in January stated that Mr. Sheppard would attempt to break his own record on Sunday January 21st. An advertising announcement on 3rd February stated that an anonymous challenger had come forward and that Mr. Sheppard had

stood down to give him a chance. The attempt would be made on the following day, Sunday 4th. The event was supported by several Isle of Wight motor dealers and the record was duly broken. The following Saturday *The County Press* reported the record broken when the rider went through a tunnel of burning straw 80 feet long, beating Dick Sheppard's 65ft 7$\frac{1}{2}$in from the previous year at Shanklin. In true mystery man fashion the rider leapt into a speedboat after his ride and was whisked away without revealing his identity.

A brochure for the marina from 1973 still refers to the former name Medway Queen Marina! The postal address of the marina and ships was given as East Medina Mill although that no longer existed. Press advertising for the two ships had been using the Wight Marina name since the previous May. In 1973 the boatel and catering was managed by Gardner Merchant Food Services Ltd. in association with Wight Marina. Gardner Merchant were part of the Trust House Forte Group.

Through the first months of 1973 the Miss Wight Marina 1973 Beauty Contest continued and, according to *County Press* reports, it was won by Valerie Cole of Binstead. The musical attractions included Dave Allington's Disco, the Eric Stevens Trio (Funnel Bar) and Dancing to Pseudo Foot. In the Boiler Bar, Dave's performance was, again, enlivened by the Ryde Queen Go-Go Girls. The Keel Bar was advertised in this year but the name was dropped for 1974. In addition to the regular discos and dances, rooms were let out for meetings and wedding receptions were catered for. In the run-up to Christmas a party for children from residential homes on the island was held, funded by an earlier charity event on board. No other Christmas advertising has been discovered. There was little trouble from customers, drunk or otherwise, and only a very few instances made it into the local press. Those few were mostly in the car park – the ship's bouncers keeping a tight control over their own patch.

In August 1973 ATV used the marina as a location for filming scenes for a *Life of King Edward VII* series. The series was based on the biography by Sir Phillip Magnus. Although *PS Ryde* was not used in the filming the older vessel, *PS Medway Queen*, appeared in the background of some scenes. The King was played by Timothy West and in one scene he was seen greeting Princess Alexandra, played by Deborah Grant, on her arrival from Denmark.

In 1974 a scheme for further expansion of the marina ran into opposition from Newport Borough Council and advertising for the two ships did not start until May. They re-opened under the management of Reynolds and Gaywood Associates. Quentin Reynolds and Paul Gaywood owned the business, leasing the two ships and the marina from the Ridett family. Quentin Reynolds knew how to make entertainment work and he organised that aspect of the business while Paul Gaywood handled the financial side. A three panel advertisement in *The County Press* for May 18th included Wight Marina, *Medway Queen* Night Club and Ryde Queen Boatel. The marina, it said, was open for business after major repair work and carried re-assurance that *Medway Queen* and *Ryde Queen* would not be leaving the island. An ambitious sounding line–up was promised with a noticeable shift towards drag acts and cabaret. A definite shift in emphasis, perhaps to target a wider audience than the marina clients and their families. Private functions including wedding receptions continued to be welcomed.

The *Medway Queen* Club had DJs Spike Davis and Mad Malc augmented by acts billed as "Top London cabaret and drag acts" with The Mosaics on Thursday 23rd May and Perri St. Clair the following week. On board the Ryde Queen Boatel there was a Grand Opening Dance with The Shantones and Mike Gordine. On weekdays music was provided by Quorum with Lee Dean on Wednesdays, Thursdays and Fridays. The features advertised were a restaurant, accommodation, two bars, cabaret, modern dancing and live music. On *Medway Queen*, standards were maintained with an announcement that "no person under 21 years admitted (unless accompanied). No jeans, cords, T-shirts or the like". On *Ryde Queen*, gentlemen were requested to wear a collar and tie. The advertisement erroneously referred to two Dunkirk paddle steamers moored in the marina.

There was a continued level of advertising in *The County Press* and charity events began to appear later in the year. In November there were fund raising evenings for Ginger Bread and for the Isle of Wight Society for Mentally Handicapped Children. The charity events took place on Tuesdays (Quentin Reynolds ran the bar himself on these nights) with cabaret acts on the Wednesday. On November 20th a novelty act in the form of the Buckmaster Puppet Show was advertised. Michael Buckmaster toured with a specialty act which presented much loved trick marionettes and delighted audiences at variety performances, cabaret venues, holiday camps, social clubs and theatres around Britain from 1948 – 1999. Mike's most popular acts were his unique versions of the disjointing skeleton, the Grand Turk, the striptease puppet, the juggling unicyclist, the trampoline and the flying trapeze figures, famous celebrities in miniature and his original invention of three-tier puppetry – a puppeteer working a puppet working a puppet. He had previously appeared on Thursday 28th February 1974 on *Medway Queen*; the timing of that act meant that he missed the last ferry home and stayed overnight in a cabin on board the *Ryde Queen*.

There was a B&B business with the cabins in the aft part of the ship and the restaurant. Spike Davis remembers Rosalind Murphy who was always working and also managed the St. Helens café. Spike and Rosalind ran the B&B for a season. A dinner dance in aid of the Isle of Wight Society for Mentally Handicapped Children in November was attended by over 180 people and raised £120 for the society; not bad in those days. The event included an auction, competition and a cabaret performance by Australian singer Tina St. Clair. A further £130 was presented to the society by The Sunday Club at the event. In December a Night of Entertainment was held in aid of the British Heart Foundation. The £1 ticket included a meal of chicken and chips. A further event in December in aid of the BHF was Grand Christmas Stag Night with DJ Spike Davis, cabaret and Tom Bennett on the Hammond Organ. No other Christmas events were advertised but there was a party for children from the island's residential homes.

The *Medway Queen* Club finally closed at the end of 1974 and did not reopen the following year, leaving the *Ryde Queen* as the only entertainment venue at the marina. The discos moved to *Ryde Queen* and there was, apparently, a wind-up gramophone as backup for the disco.

The level of advertising and press reports began to dwindle in 1975. In March there was a small ad and display advertisement for hen and stag parties with cabaret acts and strippers. These became a staple in the *Ryde Queen*'s schedule and, according to some reports, they could be held on the same nights and guests at the two events would mingle. Spike Davis ran hamburger bars on *Ryde Queen* and on Sandown Sea front. Charity events continued in this year and in March there was a fund-raising evening with cabaret for Cowes Carnival Committee where 200 guests raised about £129 for the carnival funds. Further events for the carnival were held later in the year and in November there was a disco for the Sea Cadets.

A *Medway Queen* Club Reunion Dance was held on board *Ryde Queen* at Easter 1975, the year after the *Medway Queen* Club closed. Ticket (*below*) courtesy of Quentin Reynolds.

Although event advertising fell away the venue continued to place small ads for staff as circumstances required which suggests an increasing reliance on regular clients who returned repeatedly without a need for expenditure on advertising. Advertised events became less frequent and the business ticked over on a predictable schedule. There may well have been advertising by other means such as

Crested china depicting *Medway Queen* and *Ryde Queen* and used on both vessels in the early 1970s.
Top Left: plate and saucer (*Richard Halton*)
Top Right: coffee pot (*PSPS Collection*)
Bottom Right: tea pot (*Stella Bassett*).

leaflets or posters. There were also regular entries in the dancing list advertisements in the local paper.

Mark Earp remembers working on board The Boat in the mid-1970s. It was his local nightclub and, as an "impoverished student", he funded his visits by working there from time to time; clearing tables or managing the cloakroom. He remembers that security was in the hands of Ginger Knight who worked on a local farm by day and on the *Ryde Queen* in the evenings. He recalled a number of incidents from his times on board. On occasion, as the boat was in a tidal lagoon, the vessel would lean to starboard at quite an angle as the tide ebbed.   Dancers and glasses would go flying. A lady once dropped a ring into the open engine room; when a ladder went down and a torch was beamed into the bowels of the boat one could see swarms of rats living in the bilges. In a long hot summer in the mid-1970s it was so stifling hot while dancing on the boat that many revellers ran down to the River Medina to swam in the river and cool down. Mark swam across the river to make his way home.

Mark also remembers an occasion when the police boarded the vessel and secured all routes of disembarkation. eight handbags had gone missing. They kept well over 100 revellers secured on board for four hours and searched the whole ship thoroughly. Eventually the people were allowed to leave as nothing had been found! The following morning at low tide the handbags were all found stuck in the mud of the lagoon outside the female toilets' window.

Through 1976, the pattern continued. A fund-raising night for Cowes Carnival Committee on March 30th featured Lee Sutton, billed as a "top London drag artist". There was a slight increase in Magistrates Court references to *Ryde Queen* in 1976 including an incident in the car park in February and a scuffle on board later. The latter resulted in a court appearance in July when an assault case was dismissed. Advertising seems to veer away from the boatel and towards a floating pub or floating nightclub description. The boatel cabins were not regularly let out but might be offered to customers in the event of bad weather making homeward journeys difficult. One lady who contacted us remembered being offered one in heavy snow but since she and her companion were only on a first date they declined.

The boatel featured briefly in a novel set in that year. In Isabel Ashdown's novel Summer of '76 the main character, Luke, with a few friends visits the club. The author describes *Ryde Queen* as "magnificent with the huge red funnel protruding skywards". According to this fictional account the décor was a little garish and run down by then but their tour of the ship took in the engine room with its "Perspex viewing wall", the Normandy Lounge with its sixties sounds and the Admiral's Disco. These names, of course, relate to the use of compartments a little later in the ship's career, as does the funnel colour.

Linda McCully, who worked behind the bar in the 1970s, up to the time of the 1977 fire, remembers the charity nights and the effective bouncers. The Wednesday cabaret acts included Mrs. Shufflewick (Rex Jameson from The Black

The Ryde Queen Boatel from the river side.

Cap, Camden) and the Hinge and Bracket musical drag duo (George Logan and Patrick Fyffe). Spike Davis (DJ) remembers that the piano stool had to be raised with a copy of a telephone directory for "Dame Hilda" of Hinge and Bracket. Linda recalls a preponderance of drag acts. The routine was that staff would arrive at 9pm to set up. Most lived locally due to transport difficulties when going home after work. The manager would open up and all would be ready by 10pm but it didn't usually get busy until around 11pm after the pubs closed. Linda also recalled working in the Funnel bar on Friday/Saturday nights with the Eric Stevens Trio playing there. She also remembered that the boatel cabins were occasionally used by staff or friends. At one time, due to licensing requirements, the bar was separated by a grill and customers had to order drinks and have them delivered to their table.

There was a staff newsletter, produced by Sue Murphy, with caricatures of the people involved and a high level of gossip content. Among incidents remembered were one Thursday before Easter when they had to close at 12 because they had been unable to get a drinks licence for Good Friday and one exceptionally high tide when the ship heeled over and the gangways rose too high forcing the club to close. Sue Murphy was also the resident singer and the sister of Rosalind who managed the boatel and restaurant.

In 1977 press advertising reduced even more but small display advertisements in March promoted Striptease Shows every Wednesday. The business suffered when the licensing laws were tightened; opening hours were cut back and the police began to target the area for drink-driving violations. Other clubs on the Island were affected too. Some *Ryde Queen* staff lived on the *Regal Queen* houseboat moored nearby, Quentin had quarters on the upper deck and Spike had a small flat on the lower deck.

In April there was an advertisement for a disco in aid of the Isle of Wight Yacht Club Silver Jubilee Appeal. A larger display advertisement in July described the *Ryde Queen* as The Island's Floating Nightclub and announced that it was open every night, 9pm to 2am (Sunday midnight). DJs Marc Antony and Dave Cass were featured with live music in the Funnel Bar on Fridays and Saturdays with the Eric Stevens Trio. Admission was 50p and nobody under 21 was admitted. There was a Sunday Lunchtime Special from 12 to 3pm and cabaret and striptease on Wednesdays. The Marlboro Disco was advertised for Thursday July 28th. Interestingly, although boatel had dropped from the headline it still apeared as the address at the bottom of the advertisement.

The overall business (Wight Marina Co.) had been in the hands of the liquidators for some time by August 1977, with Alan Ridett acting on their behalf. In the early morning of 10th August 1977 *Ryde Queen* suffered a mysterious fire which closed the club. Linda McCully was working on the ship on the night of the fire; everything was locked up as usual at the end of the open time and the staff went home as normal. It is thought that the fire started on the lower deck at about 3:30am and it was seen by two men fishing from the river bank who saw flames around the funnel of the ship. They called the fire brigade and the police. Paul Gaywood and the assistant manager were asleep on board and the first they knew of it was when a police officer woke them up! More than 60 firemen fought the blaze for two hours to bring it under control. Fire appliances from Newport, Cowes, East Cowes, Ryde, Sandown and Shanklin were called to the incident. It was later found that furniture appeared to have been stacked to accelerate the fire and this must have happened after the staff had gone home. A number of rumours circulated regarding the fire and its cause but no proof was ever found and no charges levelled. It remains a mystery. The fire had spread through 3 decks destroying bars and the dance floor and damage was estimated at around £100,000.

Two views of the fire on 10th August 1977.

Dave Cannon

The aftermath of the fire.

Dave Cannon

Dave Cannon in front of the refurbished *Ryde Queen*.

Dave Cannon Collection

Following the fire on board *Ryde Queen*, *Medway Queen* was sold in September 1977. She was bought by Jim Ashton and his associates from Kent who purchased the ship from the liquidators handling the marina's affairs. They set up a trust and patched *Medway Queen* up for a move and restoration attempt. Their efforts were rewarded in April 1984 when she was moved downstream to Cowes on a high tide. There she was taken to the CEGB jetty and floated onto a submersible salvage pontoon for her sea journey. The press reported that she left amid a fanfare of sirens and hundreds of people turned up to see the ship begin her journey home to the River Medway.

It was some time before the business, renamed Medina Yacht Harbour, re-opened. The buyer had been negotiating for almost three years when a dispute over repair costs had been settled and the purchase agreed early in 1978. Barclay Russell, a director of the Liltwain Company, explained his ambitious plans for the marina to the press in February 1978. They hoped to provide leisure facilities that would attract visitors to Binfield. The *Ryde Queen* would re-open and 51 detached holiday chalets would be built. The first phase with 11 chalets was now the subject of a full planning application and a later application would be made for an open air heated swimming pool and possibly tennis and squash courts. This planning application and a later, even more ambitious one, was denied by the Medina Borough Council because of concerns for the rural area, a nearby site of special scientific interest and the council's own plans for a Medina Waterpark along the river bank. The marina was, yet again, denied the development that was needed to ensure financial viability.

The relationship of the parties involved in the purchase and attempted development of the marina appears complex. Liltwain was formed in order to purchase and run the *Ryde Queen* although the marina development planning application was also made in their name. A separate company was then set up to run the marina under the name Medina Yacht Harbour. Liltwain purchased the marina and *Ryde Queen* from the liquidator in 1978 and applied for VAT registration in October 1980. In November of that year Liltwain's assets were purchased by the Medina Yacht Harbour Company with Barclay Russell continuing to operate *Ryde Queen* on their behalf. A formal tenancy agreement was concluded in March 1981 but this lasted only until November 1982 when Barclay Russell gave up the tenancy. Liltwain was formally dissolved the following year. A VAT control visit in March 1983 resulted in the discovery of VAT irregularities to the tune of £7817, accrued during the tenancy period, for which Barclay Russell was found liable and which he was forced to correct.

The repair estimate for *Ryde Queen* had been reduced to £50000 and work was already underway, much of it we now know being undertaken by Dave Cannon who had a long association with the two paddle steamers as both DJ and maintenance man. *Ryde Queen*'s licence had already been transferred from Quentin Reynolds to Mr. Russell, and it was hoped that the ship would reopen in May 1978, although the exact nature of facilities to be offered had not been decided. The boatel cabins were removed, however, to make way for a new restaurant.

The first press advertisements found for the re-opened *Ryde Queen* were in September 1978 and the venue was marketed as *Paddle Steamer Ryde Queen*. There was the

The main restaurant became a lounge bar after the fire. Taken from the DJ's desk with Barclay Russell behind the bar.

Dave Cannon

Upper deck, aft saloon fitted out as restaurant.

Dave Cannon

new restaurant and many of the bars etc. had new names. The Admiral's Disco with resident DJ Beau Jangles in the Normandy Bar was advertised for every Wednesday from 11th October. It would be open from 9pm to 1am. Hot and cold snacks would be available during all opening hours including lunch times (12 noon to 3pm). The annual membership fee for the club was £10 for individual membership or £15 for a married couple. Daily membership 75p, 50p on Mondays and Tuesdays. Once again the display advertisements used an old name for the marina; Wight Marina. In fact the name Medina Yacht Harbour was not used on *Ryde Queen* advertising for several years. The main deck was variously referred to as Main Deck, Centre Deck and, later, Normandy Deck. In 1980 the Admiral's Disco was advertised as on the Normandy Deck and the Normandy Bar was advertised from September 1978 to October 1980.

Ryde Queen's turn to star in a film came in 1979. *The Wildcats of St. Trinian's* was partly filmed at the marina in that year and includes a clear shot of *Medway Queen* apparently still afloat at her berth. Quite a few scenes, including the customary St. Trinian's "battle" were filmed on *Ryde Queen*, mostly on the promenade deck, with a water-borne assault (using a variety of very unsuitable craft) attacking across the river. Some of the staff including Sue Murphy, who had worked on *Ryde Queen* for years, also worked on the film. Other scenes had been filmed on the Isle of Wight at locations such as Sandown esplanade and beach, and Norris Castle. The World Charity Premiere of the film was screened at Newport's Community Theatre on Wednesday 9th April 1980 and the film is now available on YouTube.

Also in 1979 eight fourth year students from Carisbrooke High School in Newport undertook an Industrial Archaeology project on board *Ryde Queen*. They were studying science and technology at the school and did the work as part of that course. They worked on the mechanical parts including major repairs in the engine room which had been damaged in the fire. They cleared out layers of cinders and ash, removed heavy coats of rust and made some replacement parts. The ship's owner supplied all materials necessary and their eventual aim was to get the engine turning over under electrical power. This was estimated as a five year project but, sadly, there is no indication that this aim was ever achieved. Nevertheless it gave the students the opportunity to undertake tasks and use materials that would not otherwise have been possible.

In April 1980 the ship was advertised as Open Nightly except Sunday and Monday with Golden Oldies on the Normandy Deck and Admiral's Disco on the lower deck. On Sundays there was family lunchtime entertainment with the Brian Martin Trio on the Normandy Deck and a Kiddies Disco (for under 15s) on the Lower Deck. One can imagine the reaction of today's 12 to 15 year olds to a "Kiddies Disco"! Sunday lunchtime opening was from 12:30 to 3:30 with food served from 1pm.

In 1981 the line-up was modified with Music of the '50s and '60s by DJ Dave Cannon on Wednesdays and Music and Dancing of Yesteryear on Thursday to Saturday on the Centre Deck, again with Dave Cannon. Bob Wells' disco was sighted on the Lower Deck. This style of entertainment continued through 1981 with the addition, towards the end of the year, of "Opportunity knocks-Knock it back" on Thursday 19th November. Reported charity support for the Wessex Body Scanner Appeal included nearly £200 raised

The quality of work carried out by the pupils of Carisbrooke High School can be readily appreciated from this image.
Gordon Pavey, courtesy of his son, Andrew

at a disco organised by The Wallies in May and £30 at an Elvis Night, attended by 120 fans, for an evening of music and films in August.

Since September 1980 Medina Yacht Harbour had been under the control of Keith Webb. Plans for a new control tower for the marina were initially put before the planning committee in 1981. After rejection and a war of words, the plans were approved later in the year. The tower was (and still is) a mushroom shaped, modern design, incorporating offices and the lock entry controls for the marina. Work was soon under way to enlarge and improve the facilities and early in 1982 further plans were approved for additional mooring pontoons, a new carpark with landscaping and a new access road for the *Ryde Queen*'s customers. The marina would have berthing facilities for 300 craft ranging in length from 20ft to 60ft. The additional trade could only benefit *Ryde Queen*.

In 1982 the *Ryde Queen*'s offering was much the same as in the previous year although there was little press advertising. A group called The Choir was advertised in January. The focus seems to have been daytime snacks or light meals and evening discos for the whole of this period. In effect reverting to the original concept of the ship as part of the marina's facilities and aimed at the boat owners and their families. There was a Christmas Eve disco with Dave Cannon's and Rob Wells' discos and a New Year's Eve Fancy Dress event.

The advertising, and presumably the business, picked up in 1983. In March advertisements included Sound FX and

Fire Damage. This leaflet had been used behind panelling as packing. The singed holes are from heat conducted by the nails.

Dave Cannon

Paddle Steamer RYDE. Portsmouth–Ryde Route in British Rail colours

Medina Yacht Harbour, Binfield, Newport, Isle of Wight (0983) 526733

Dave Cannon Collection

The Stigma as well as the two regular DJs and their discos. The marina re-opened from 2nd April with the silhouette of the mushroom control tower proudly depicted on the display advert. The *Ryde Queen* advertised the Garage Band for Thursday 21st April and was open on Sunday lunchtimes with guitarist Robert Kross. From May the ship offered over 21s discos on Thursdays, Fridays and Saturdays and the Boiler Room Disco on Fridays and Saturdays only. On Sunday Robert Kross continued to entertain the lunchtime diners. DJ Beau Jangles was back in the Marina Bar from July and now billed as a former entertainer with P&O luxury liners. The crowds attracted were large enough to cause concern over the stability of the forward main deck. Visitors in the lower saloon became aware that the deckhead above them was flexing due to the number of dancers and additional supports had to be added below. Whether this was due to the removal of bulkheads in 1972 or weakening by fire damage in 1977 is unknown.

On Saturday 10th August the annual raft race on the River Medina raised about £600 for the Newport branch of the RNLI. The race started by the *Ryde Queen* with 10 rafts taking part. There were some 400 spectators and crews

from the RNLI, local companies, police and prison officers. The winner was a raft made of oil drums and entered by the Vikoma International Marine Engineering Company of Cowes. In second place was another raft from the same company with third place going to a team of Albany Prison Officers. The winning time was 28 minutes with the last raft completing the course in a time of an hour and a half.

There was an effort in 1984 to revive the club and build on the 1983 results. From February discos were advertised as free on Fridays but an admission fee was charged on Saturdays. In March there was a Bottled Gas Use trade exhibition, organised by Medina Leisure Park who had been appointed as distributor by ACC Gases & Shell UK. The event was reported as well attended on 13th April by the Isle of Wight County Press. The *Ryde Queen* Club closed for renovations in early April although a further trade exhibition, for copiers, was held on 21st and 22nd April.

The announced plan was to re-open at Easter but it was 27th April before the new Millers Bistro and Coffee Shop opened for business on board the paddle steamer. This was open on Friday, Saturday and Sunday evenings and at lunch time on Saturday and Sunday only. An advertised

Medina Yacht Harbour promotion.

Dave Cannon Collection

feature was the view of the original engines and other equipment and the vessel's history. On 4th May a new night club was announced and notice given that a disco by Juliana's of London (for over 18s) would open on the Lower Deck shortly. The re-opening was on 11th May with Juliana's International Discotheque on the Lower Deck and the Binnacle Bar and the new nightclub for over 25s on the main deck. It is unclear whether Juliana's was a sub contract, franchise or equipment hire organisation. Ian Mac joined the DJ team of Dave Cannon and Rob Wells at about this time. This pattern was followed through the year with an RNLI Fun day and Regatta (with raft race) on 17th July and the return of live jazz with the Unity Stompers in November. This advertised free admission for ladies but the Equal Opportunities Commission found that it contravened the 1975 Sexual Discrimination Act. Ladies had to pay thereafter.

Juliana's disappeared around the end of 1984 amid rumours of unpaid bills for the hire of their equipment and the club continued as before advertising the Ryde Queen Night Club and Disco at Medina Yacht Harbour. The RNLI held their regatta in June and the description changed again in the summer months to floating pub – no doubt to attract casual visitors from the ranks of the Isle of Wight's holiday makers. In October the line-up was an Over 25s club on Thursdays with a German Wine Promotion on Friday October 25th and a Whitbread Best Bitter event the following week.

Press advertising reduced again in 1985/86 and Keith Webb apparently came to the conclusion that too few people were chasing too many nightclubs. He was

appointed as the trustee for Medina Yacht Harbour which was in financial trouble again and sold out in 1987 to a company called Waterspace, which had been incorporated on 7th April. The marina name changed to Island Harbour. Activity on the *Ryde Queen* continued in the same pattern. In March 1987 a sponsored disco by two girls (Michelle and Joanne) raised £60 with a further £60, from a competition run on board, for toys donated to Children's Ward St Mary's Hospital charity. The RNLI regatta was held in June and a series of antiques and collectors fairs started in December.

Advertising in November proclaimed that Friday is Jazz and Blues night with the Chuff Train Stompers and the musical talents of Brian Charles. The resident DJ was billed as Ian. On Christmas Eve Dave Cannon's Solent City Sound disco was on offer along with the resident DJ and for New Year's Eve a "Daring Disco" was promised. A "beat a breathalyser" coach service was run to Newport Bus Station at the end of the evening.

The *Ryde Queen* Club formally closed at the end of the 1987 New Year's Eve event with a surprise announcement, but a bar remained open on the Main Deck, primarily for the use of boat owners. The collectors' fairs continued on board from time to time and in June 1989 live music by the Peter Hogman Band was advertised for every Friday and Midnight Blue every Saturday. The timing suggests that this was intended for the holiday season when the marina would be busiest.

Island Harbour has changed hands a number of times since the *Ryde Queen* closed, with its current owners taking over on 2nd January 2013. Frequent changes of ownership and business uncertainty, with periods in the

Dave Cannon and Solent City Sound on *Ryde Queen* in 1981.

Dave Cannon Collection

Ryde Queen door staff in the 1980s.

Dave Cannon

Dave Cannon Collection

hands of receivers, may be one reason why efforts to preserve the vessel and restore her have faltered. The overriding factor, however, has to be a lack of funding; restoring a ship is expensive and unlikely to ever make a true financial return. Like the steam railways, subsidies in the forms of volunteer labour and cash donations are always needed. In today's market a ship the size of PS *Ryde*, no longer watertight or structurally sound and firmly aground some yards from the river, would probably require a budget in the region of £10M-£15M for restoration, plus a considerable volunteer input. The survival of the bones of the old ship to the present day (2020) is due to the lower, but still significant, sum needed just to remove her. Two serious preservation attempts have been made, however.

In 1991, when they learned that the owners wished to dispose of PS *Ryde*, the Paddle Steamer Preservation Society took an interest and formed a *Ryde* Project Sub-Committee to look into possible restoration opportunities. The move was supported by the operating companies of PS *Waverley* and PS *Kingswear Castle*, although these organisations would not be able to provide financial support. The Chairman of the *Medway Queen* Preservation Society was kept informed and he and the *Medway Queen* Foundation Director, Peter Bowring, contributed to the plan. The *Medway Queen* Foundation had been formed and registered as a charity in 1991 to support restoration of that ship but was closed down by March 2009. PS *Ryde* was the last surviving Denny-built paddle steamer and hopes were high for a successful project.

Over the next year or so PSPS volunteers fought to refloat PS *Ryde*. The owning company paid for materials and the volunteers laboriously removed and replaced defective plating. The work rate increased significantly when a jig was designed and constructed to ease the fitting of hull plates which measured eight feet by four feet (2400mm x 1200mm). In the meantime PSPS members had pledged a total of £106,000 to the project and the plan was to offer that money to the owners of the ship as a loan to help fund professional restoration in a shipyard. There were plans to re-open the ship in a static museum role but these were deferred as the work timescales increased.

In June 1992 MV *Balmoral* made two visits to the River Medina so that her passengers could view PS *Ryde*. On the first occasion (June 6th) vintage coaches were run from Newport to bring passengers down to Island Harbour for a closer look. The second visit was about a week later and took place after dark. The volunteers lit up PS *Ryde* for the occasion and that was much appreciated by MV *Balmoral*'s passengers. The ship's steering engine and the aft capstan with its engine were removed for use on PS *Waverley*. PS *Ryde*'s future was seen as a static exhibit, at least in the short to medium term so this would not have been a problem.

PS *Ryde* refloated on the spring tides of August and September 1992. There was a still small leak in the hull but that was contained between the two remaining functional bulkheads. The sensation of the ship moving on the tide was very much appreciated by the volunteers who had made it possible. The owning company announced a plan to open in 1993 with catering facilities on board but relations between them and PSPS had cooled and the volunteer project was withdrawn. No record that this scheme to run a catering establishment actually came to fruition has been found.

In 1994 excursions were advertised by MV *Balmoral* and PS *Waverley* in connection with the 50th anniversary of D-Day. Departures from Yarmouth Pier for various cruises were advertised for 29th, 30th and 31st May and for 4th June. MV *Balmoral*'s cruise on May 31st left Yarmouth at 2pm to *"cruise up the fascinating River Medina to salute the*

Dave Cannon Collection

Martin Hall Collection

Veteran D-Day paddle steamer Ryde which served at the Normandy landings". Fares were £9 with a discounted fare of £7.95 for senior citizens and D-Day veterans.

The Paddle Steamer Preservation Society stayed in contact with the successive owners of PS *Ryde* and Island Harbour Marina over the years and with Mark Young who began a campaign to save PS *Ryde* in 2002. He undertook considerable research into the ship's history and built a website with images of PS *Ryde* donated by many enthusiasts. The restoration cost estimate was, according to press reports in 2004, £7 million. This led to the formation of the Paddle Steamer *Ryde* Trust, registered as a charity in 2010. The PSPS continued to explore options for the ship with the owners, and had met with them in 2006, but were never able to reach agreement on a selling price. Competitive offers hoped for by the owners never came to anything and the ship continued to deteriorate. PSPS encouraged the Paddle Steamer *Ryde* Trust and made space available to them in their journal, *Paddle Wheels*. A comprehensive restoration plan was commissioned, but sadly the required high level of funding was never forthcoming.

In 2009/10 dismantling of the ship was about to take place without the knowledge of those trying to save her. The vessel was, again, in the hands of receivers following a bankruptcy. The PSPS contacted the Isle of Wight Council, National Historic Ships UK and the Environment Agency and work stopped on the order of the Environment Agency and the Health and Safety Executive. The ship was reprieved (again) but a sale for preservation could still not be negotiated.

The current owners have been sympathetic to preservation of the old ship. They obtained a stay of execution from the Isle of Wight Council's Planning Department with permission to retain the vessel for another three years. The Paddle Steamer *Ryde* Trust continued to lobby and late in 2018 a new scheme was launched under the auspices of ship restoration company Siward & Co. An appeal was started to fund surveys and the Paddle Steamer *Ryde* Trust prepared to hand over to the restoration company but nothing came of this plan. Inspection of the ship showed that there would be considerable problems relating to environmental issues as well as the need to dismantle on site in order to remove the remains. That in itself will be a costly exercise. Siward pulled out after a fairly short period of involvement and remaining money from the survey fund was passed to the *Medway Queen* Preservation Society as had been promised. The one positive result of this episode was that it sparked a completely separate historical research project leading to this publication.

There is still a possibility that PS *Ryde*'s engine will be preserved as a museum exhibit. National Historic Ships UK and the Paddle Steamer Preservation Society are investigating this. The engine console and one ventilator from the ship are already in the PSPS collection. The aft capstan still serves on PS *Waverley* but sadly the steering engine was removed. Various other artefacts do still exist in museums and elsewhere and interest has been shown in acquiring others when the ship is dismantled. Perhaps some reminder will even be retained by Island Harbour Marina as an onsite memorial to this beautiful old ship.

An entry in the Ryde Carnival Parade promoting the Elvis nights.

Another entry in the Ryde Carnival Parade in the early 1980s.

Ryde Queen in May 1981, a reminder of the happier days.
Bob Owens

PS *Ryde* began to deteriorate and the funnel collapsed in 2006. By April 2013 the ship was a sad sight.

By November 2017 the bridge and superstructure were also collapsing.

Both: Richard Halton

Two views of the once proud ship in October 2020.

John Hendy

PS *Medway Queen* at Gillingham Pier, Kent.

Richard Halton

PS *Medway Queen*'s refurbished aft saloon in 2020.

Mick Appleyard

MEDWAY QUEEN

PS *Medway Queen* and PS *Ryde* have shared more than one chapter in their history; most notably as entertainment venues at Island Harbour (at that time named Wight Marina) on the Isle of Wight. Unlike PS *Ryde*, PS *Medway Queen* was rescued after she fell out of use and taken back to the River Medway and after a change of ownership, she was eventually rebuilt with support from the Heritage Lottery Fund and the European Regional Development Fund. She is now moored at Gillingham Pier, near Chatham, where her enthusiastic team of volunteers are fitting out the ship's interior.

PS *Medway Queen* was launched on 23rd April 1924 and entered service in July of that year. Her inaugural voyage was for invited guests on Friday 18th July from Strood and Chatham to Southend and then across to Herne Bay. This became her normal route but excursions were also run to Margate and Clacton. Special events and excursions were also undertaken; including the 1937 Spithead Naval Review. In 1938 PS *Medway Queen* was converted to oil-firing. This had the advantage that during the Dunkirk evacuation she could refuel far more quickly and easily than her coal fired sisters.

After assisting with the evacuation of children in 1939, PS *Medway Queen* was converted for minesweeping and fitted with a 12pdr gun on the forward deck and machine guns on the paddle boxes. The aft saloon was cut down; providing more deck space for the minesweeping gear and the bridge was strengthened. HMS *Medway Queen* was commissioned in November 1939 and went to Harwich. She later joined the 10th minesweeping flotilla in Dover.

The official order for Operation Dynamo, the evacuation from Dunkirk, was issued on Sunday 26th May although some troops had already been evacuated. On HMS *Medway Queen*'s first trip (27th May) everything was chaotic; the ships anchored offshore and used their boats to collect men from the beaches - a slow process. As Dynamo proceeded HMS *Medway Queen* settled into a routine; each night was filled with the noise and danger of battle and the following day was spent clearing up and replenishing fuel and stores. As well as the danger it was physically exhausting. The French rearguard was picked up on the night of 3rd June. While loading, a ship astern of HMS *Medway Queen* was hit and driven into the paddle box causing some damage. Repairs were made in Portsmouth and the ship served as a minesweeper for the remainder of the war – a story in itself – moving to a training establishment in Edinburgh in 1944.

After the war she was refitted in Southampton and resumed her old route under Captain Leonard Horsham. The summer seasons followed a similar pattern to those before the war with excursions and charters mixed in. In 1953 she attended the Coronation Review at Spithead in the official line up and with a full complement of passengers. PS *Medway Queen* continued in service until the end of the 1963 season when she was withdrawn.

After a number of schemes had been tried to save the ship a sale was arranged to a Belgian ship breaker and PS *Medway Queen* was prepared for the cross channel

journey. Fortunately the company was sympathetic to the history of the vessel and when Alan Ridett offered to buy the ship for use on the Isle of Wight they willingly cooperated. PS *Medway Queen* was towed to the island, arriving in Cowes on 28th September 1965. The ceremonial opening of the *Medway Queen* Club took place on Saturday May 14th 1966.

The club flourished as both restaurant and nightclub but eventually maintenance needs outpaced business profits and the club closed in 1974. In 1984 the ship was moved back to the river Medway for preservation. The *Medway Queen* Preservation Society was formed in 1985 to assist that project but became owners of the ship in 1987. After many years at Damhead Creek on the Isle of Grain a grant by the Heritage Lottery Fund enabled the hull rebuild in Bristol and in 2013 she returned to a mooring on Gillingham Pier where she is being fitted out by a small but enthusiastic volunteer team.

The first stage of the refit was to make the ship usable as a venue which could be hired out for events. By the end of 2020 that stage was almost complete but proceedings were slowed by the effects of the Corona virus. The main deck saloons have been refitted in an appropriate style, the galley equipped with modern appliances to meet current hygiene regulations. Fire alarms and other safety features have been installed.

Read More: The history of *Medway Queen* and her rebuild has been published by the society in a number of books and in summary on the society's website:

www.medwayqueen.co.uk

Contact the society at Gillingham Pier, Pier Approach Road, Gillingham, Kent. ME7 1RX. Help in all forms, practical, managerial and financial is desperately needed to keep this project moving forward. Your purchase of this book has helped but can you do more?

SOURCES & ACKNOWLEDGEMENTS

Acknowledgements

Many individuals, far more than I even hoped for, have come forward and offered help. That help has been in the form of their own research notes, personal recollections and (to my relief) literally hundreds of photographs; far more than we have space for. But that is a better problem than not having enough. Considerable amounts of information, help and photographs were received from the following people who raided their notes and archives on my behalf: Dave Cannon (Solent City Sound), Darren Cooke, John Goss, David Green (PSPS), John Hendy, Chris King, Mark Ridett, Graham Shaw and Mark Young (PS *Ryde* Trust). I must also thank Ivan Berryman and Rod Williams for permission to include their paintings.

More information and/or images were received from: John Allen (PSPS), Mick Appleyard, Isabel Ashdown, Stella Bassett, Peter Box, Richard Brierly, Fred Caws, Roger Caws, Tim Cooper, Paul (Spike) Davis, Barry J Eagles, Mark Earp, Margaret Elcombe, Ray Farrow, Barry J Finch, Linda Fry, John Fulford, Derek Gawn, Andy Gilbert (ournewhaven website), Gregory Gould, Great Central Railway Auctions, Martin Hall, Lewis Harper, John Hulse, Robin Jones, Jackie Keen, Nigel Lawrence, Jenni Le Mouton, Ian Mac, Fraser MacHaffie, Andrew Munn, Susan O'Halloran, Bob Owens, Andrew Pavey, Quentin Reynolds, Richard Readings, Peter Seabroke, Chris Tebbutt, Mick Watts, Andy Westmore and Allen Young,

Without the generous assistance of all these people this book would have been considerably shorter.

Publications Consulted

Isle of Wight Here We Come, Hugh J. Compton, The Oakwood Press, 1997
Code Name Mulberry, Guy Hartcup, Pen & Sword 2011
The Medway Queen, Richard Halton, Medway Queen Preservation Society, 2013, 2014 & 2020
The Medway Queen Club, Richard Halton, Medway Queen Preservation Society, 2016
The Portsmouth – Ryde Passage, John Mackett, The Ravensbourne Press 1970
Portsmouth Paddlers in the 1960s, Graham Shaw
British Railways Shipping and Allied Fleets, W. Paul Clegg and John S. Styring, David & Charles, 1971
Paddle Steamers at War 1939-1945, Russell Plummer, GMS Enterprises, 1995
Sixty Years of Paddle Steamer Preservation, Richard Clammer, Black Dwarf Publications, 2019
His Majesty's Minesweepers, HMSO, 1943
Paddle Wheels (Magazine of the Paddle Steamer Preservation Society)
Coronation Review of the Fleet Souvenir programme (Commander-in-Chief Portsmouth, 1953)
British Railways special Joint notice P34 LWD 1953 (Spithead Review)
Swanage Railway magazine (Eric Walford account)

Public & Charitable Archives and collections

East Cowes Heritage Centre
Isle of Wight Heritage Service
Portsmouth History Centre
Southampton City Archives
National Railway Museum
Paddle Steamer Preservation Society
Museum of the Royal Navy, Portsmouth for HMS Ryde's Movement Log
Medway Queen Preservation Society
Paddle Steamer Ryde Trust
Alan Blackburn Collection (Isle of Wight Steam railway)

Websites

Isle of Wight County Press Archive: www.archive.iwcp.co.uk
Wikipedia
www.naval-history.net
www.historyinportsmouth.co.uk/events/ferries-ww2.htm
www.uboat.net/allies/warships/ship/7205.html
www.fishingboatheritage.co.uk/ky-73-cromorna-1910-19303-2/
www.paddlesteamers.info/Ryde.htm
Navy Lists: www.digital.nls.uk/british-military-lists/archive/93506066
ournewhaven: www.ournewhaven.org.uk/category_id__69.asp
Coal Hulk: www.gosporthistoryclub.org.uk/gosport-history-archive-index/growing-up-with-the-hulk